Kin

Roots of the Byrd Family Tree

Kay M. Byrd

Kin: Roots of the Byrd Family Tree
Published by Yawn's Publishing
2555 Marietta Hwy, Ste 103
Canton, GA 30114
www.yawnspublishing.com

Library of Congress Control Number: 2021911596

ISBN13: 978-1-954617-17-9

Printed in the United States

This book is dedicated to my husband, Hersey Davis Byrd, and to my two children, Sylvia Byrd Corts and Stephen Byrd – all of whom, of course, share the same ancestors, or KIN.

In addition, this book is dedicated to my husband's first cousin, Byrd McNeil Ball, who repeatedly encouraged me to finish the Byrd Family History Trilogy. Unfortunately, Byrd did not live to read the last of these three books, one of my greatest regrets.

KIN

This book is the genealogy and story of kinfolk who were related to the Mount Olive, Mississippi, Byrd family. It contains information about families who are the ancestors of Hersey Davis Byrd, my husband. It is the third book in the Byrd Family History Trilogy, which also includes *Traveling Companions* and *Oaks of Righteousness* by this author.

The information in this book was found from a number of resources, including the Internet, family papers, family stories, on-site visits, newspaper articles, and library books. Obviously, there are sure to be some discrepancies and some information based on guesses. Many ancestral records have been lost in courthouse fires or were simply never written down on paper, making it difficult to trace many births, deaths, and relocations without some measure of error.

It is hoped that reading about these ancestors will inspire the reader to appreciate the courage of settlers moving west, and the bravery of kinfolk to endure the hardships and challenges of life without many of the conveniences we enjoy today. Since slavery was a part of this heritage, it is hoped that the reader will understand that these families were products of their era. They were good, Christian people albeit misguided.

Kay M. Byrd

CONTENTS

THE BALL FAMILY

How does this Ball family relate to the Byrd family? Hattie Jane Ball was the mother of Nora Beatrice Brown who married Edward Leavell Byrd. They were the parents of Hersey Davis Byrd.

There are a number of Ball families in the United States, and some researchers trace the family back beyond the Norman Conquest in England to Normandy, France. However, this family's lineage could only be traced back to Horace Frederick Ball, a 19th century man who settled in south Mississippi. It has been difficult to locate his ancestors with any certainty. The information that follows is our best guestimate.

Horace Frederick Ball:

Horace "Frederick" Ball was born in 1822 in Cobleskill, Schoharie County, New York, and moved to the little village of Handsboro, Harrison County, Mississippi, when he was about thirty years old. He lived with other boarders in the home of a merchant, D. McBean.

Information from the internet about this little Mississippi village says that Handsboro, Harrison County, Mississippi, "was settled by people who came from the north, mostly New York State." A list of families who lived in and around the old town does **not** have the name of Horace Frederick Ball, however. [Currently, Handsboro is part of the incorporated City of Gulfport.]
[Source: *History of Harrison County Mississippi* by John H. Lang]

Early enterprises of Handsboro included cutting and selling timber, and since Frederick was a carpenter, it seems likely that Frederick would have located here where he probably found work using some of this timber.

An internet entry at Findagrave.com for Horace Frederick Ball says, "H. F. Ball, a master carpenter and eventually a building contractor, was active in the early days of the Village of Handsboro, MS. Contract records show he and his business partner and father-in-law, Hubbard Crawfoot, were instrumental in the construction of the first Handsboro County Courthouse constructed 1855."
[Source: findagrave.com/memorial/143114871/horace-frederick-ball; created by Jerry Stevens]

Frederick married Sarah Jane Haywood, whose stepfather, Hubbard Crawfoot, was a millwright. They were married in Harrison County on February 14, 1854. "Sarah Jane Haywood was born in the state of Ohio in 1835, the daughter of Milton Haywood and Anna "Annie" Van Tassel. At age seventeen she left Niagara County, New York, [although it is not known why she was in New York] and migrated to Handsboro with her parents--her mother Annie and stepfather Hubbard Crawfoot," according to Jerry Stevens at findagrave.com/memorial/143103328.
[Source: findagrave.com/memorial/143114871/horace-frederick-ball; created by Jerry Stevens]

Frederick and Sarah were the parents of all boys:

1. Horace Hardy Ball, born on July 9, 1856, in Handsboro, Harrison County;
2. Forrest Ball, born in 1857 in Handsboro;
3. Fredrick M. Ball, born in 1861, and died on October 26, 1916, in Simpson County;
4. Seymour H. Ball, born in 1859 in Handsboro;
5. **Lewis B. Ball**, born March 31, 1864.

[Note: Not all researchers agree on the children. Lewis is often left out, as are Seymour and Forrest.]

Frederick died sometime before 1870 and, after his death, Sarah remarried. [The exact date of Frederick's death and the location of his grave are unknown.] Sarah married William M. Clark of Simpson County, Mississippi. For awhile the couple made their home in Simpson County and then moved to Rusk County, Texas, where four more children were born. [More on these children follows.] William and Sarah lived in Texas until their deaths.

"The last official known record for Sarah was an application for a veteran widow's pension that was submitted in 1914 from her residence declared as being Bowie Co., TX." It is unknown which husband served in the Civil War.
[Source: findagrave/memorial/143103328 by Jerry Stevens]

Sarah Jane Haywood Ball Clark died on January 10, 1916, in New Boston, Bowie County, Texas.

Children of Frederick and Sarah:

Frederick and Sarah's oldest son, Horace Hardy, moved with his mother to Simpson County. He married Rosa Ann Pauline Hilton on December 25, 1878, in Rankin County, and they eventually had ten children, all of whom were born in Simpson County:

Frederick Monroe Ball (1879-1946);
Thomas Hardy Ball (1881-1940);
William N. Ball (1883-1890);
Drewry B. Ball (1885-1956);
Carrie Ida Ball Barnett (1888-1917);
Robert Sylvester Ball (1890-1918);
Marvin Appleton Ball (1893-1925);
Milton Haywood Ball (1895-1985);
Wiley I. Ball (1897-1965);
Vernon H. Ball (1902-1913).

Horace Hardy bought a farm in Simpson County next to his mother and stepfather, and a couple of his brothers lived with him and his family for a short time. He died on February 8, 1937, at age 80, and was buried in the New Zion Cemetery in Simpson County.
[Source: findagrave/memorial/83597194/hardy-ball created by ALC]

Frederick M. Ball, born in Harrison County in 1861, also moved with his mother to Simpson County. As a young man he lived next door to his parents on the farm of his brother Hardy. He married Mary Elizabeth "Mollie" Matthews on September 2, 1886, in Simpson County, and they were the parents of six children:

Wade Hampton Ball (1887);
Troy Walter Ball (1888);
Lilia May Ball (1892);
Clarence Clifford Ball (1898);
Ernest H. Ball (1901);
Effie Ball (1906).

Frederick and Mollie lived in Crystal Springs, Mississippi, but moved to Jackson where Frederick operated a grocery store for six years prior to his death of Bright's Disease. He was buried in Harmony Cemetery in Crystal Springs, Copiah County. [Source: findagrave.com/memorial/29485543, created by Michael Moore; and

3

findagrave.com/memorial/104455003/frederick-m-ball, created by Larry Crawford]

There is little information on Forrest and Seymour Ball. They were born in Harrison County and perhaps died at a young age. [The information on their last son, Lewis, follows the children of Sarah and her second husband, William.]

Children of Sarah Haywood Ball and William Clark:

The children of Sarah and William Clark were all born in Texas. Their oldest son, "Dock" Clark married twice: First to Willie A. Gipson; Secondly to Anna Adams. He was the father of Morris Gipson Clark (1895-1989), Hall William Clark (1900 – 1978), and James William Clark (1912-2011). Dock died on July 14, 1947, at age 75, and was buried in the Fairview Cemetery in Marshall, Harrison County, Texas.

Sarah's only daughter was Ida Tabitha Clark, who married John L. Smith in 1888, and was the mother of Sarah Jane Smith (1892-1924) and Fred J. Smith (1894-1924). Ida died at age 73 on July 18, 1947, in Marshall, Texas. She was buried in the Overton City Cemetery in Overton, Texas.

Sarah and William were the parents of William Marion Clark, Jr., who died on December 25, 1957, at age 82. He married Rosa Lee Smith, and their children were: Katie L. Clark Long (1899-1986), Lois O. Clark (1905-1915), and Joseph W. Clark (1914-1915).

David "Dave" Joseph Clark married Susan "Susie" [maiden name unknown]. They had at least one child, Rose L. Clark. Dave was a farmer for awhile and then worked at a sawmill as a "lumber checker." His date of death is unknown. [Source: findagrave.com/memorial/73452445 created by D. L. Black; 93577077 created by Jerry Stevens; 5835153 Created by MB; and ancestry.com]

Lewis [or Louis] Ball:

As previously mentioned, it is not absolutely clear if Lewis was the son of Frederick and Sarah Ball. No other information is available for him, however, so we will assume this parentage.

Lewis lived in Simpson County, Mississippi, although it is unknown in which county he was born. If he was Sarah's son, as is indicated on the 1870

U. S. Census, he lived with his mother and stepfather. When the family moved to Texas, Lewis apparently did not move with them.

On the 1880 U. S. Census Lewis was seventeen years old and living on the farm owned by his brother, Horace Hardy Ball. Lewis was identified as a "laborer;" and another brother, Frederick, twenty years old, was identified as a "broker," and also living in this household. Their mother and stepfather lived two households away before their move to Texas.

On July 28, 1887, Lewis married Margaret Lou Boggan. Margaret was from a large family and was the daughter of Alexander and Nancy Jane McClendon Boggan. [More information on the Boggan family can be found in another chapter of this book.]

Lewis and Margaret soon became parents:

1. **Hattie Jane Ball**, born on May 6, 1888, in Simpson County;
2. German Washington Ball, born October 18, 1889;
3. Georgia Ball, born in 1891.

On July 16, 1892, Margaret Ball died, leaving Lewis with three young children.

On October 27 of that same year, Lewis married Mary Frances "Mollie" Williamson White, and together they had four more children. [Information about the children of Lewis and Margaret Lou Boggan follows a brief description of children of Lewis and Mollie White.]

1. Jewell Ball, born December 3, 1895, in Simpson County, died May 18, 1986 in Hinds County, Mississippi;
2. Dan Ball, born in 1897, but the date of his death is unknown;
3. Byron Preston Ball, born January 1, 1898, died on December 21, 1966;
4. Mercer Ball, born about 1908; died on December 26, 1919.

Lewis Ball owned his farm which was mortgaged but sometime around 1907 or 1908 Lewis died. The cause of his death and location of burial are unknown.

[Note: Some researchers list his death (by sepsis) in Memphis City Hospital with burial in Jackson, Mississippi. On the Tennessee Death

Certificate, this man was listed as "single." This does not seem likely since our Lewis was from Simpson County and likely was buried near his home. Also, why would a father with a wife and six children and a farm to run be as far away from Simpson County as Memphis, Tennessee?]

Mollie is listed in the 1910 census as a widow and with Mercer (who was 1½ years old), Jewell, and Byron, living with her. She made a living as a "washwoman." She was 45 years old.

Children of Lewis and Mollie:

In 1918, Lewis and Mollie's oldest son, Jewell, was drafted and served in World War I from August 8, 1918, until January 11, 1919. He was assigned to the 138th Field Artillery Brigade and trained at Camp Shelby in Hattiesburg, Mississippi. He was shipped to France on October 6, 1918, on the *Carmania,* but apparently Jewell's unit did not engage in war, or at least not for long. The Armistice was signed on November 11, 1918, and Jewell's unit was sent to the Le Mans Embarkation Center preparing to return to the United States. The regiment sailed from Brest, France, and returned to Camp Mills on Long Island, New York.

When he returned home from war, Jewell lived with Mary Ball in Jackson according to the 1920 census. He was twenty years old and his occupation was listed as "none."

By the 1930 census Jewell had married Jimmie Hardy and had one son, Louis H. Ball. Jewell began working for the United States Postal Service and continued this employment for forty years. He was a member of the Parkway Baptist Church in Jackson, Mississippi, and a Master Mason with Pearl Masonic Lodge No. 23. In addition, he was a member of the American Legion, the National Association of Retired Federal Employees, and the Disabled American Veterans.

Jewell died on May 18, 1986 and was buried in Cedarlawn Cemetery in Jackson.

In the 1900 census another son of Lewis and Molly, Dan Ball, was three years old, making his date of birth in 1897. He was not on the 1910 census. It is assumed he died as a young child.

Yet another son of Lewis and Mollie, Byron Preston Ball, was born on January 1, 1898, and lived to adulthood. He registered for World War I but apparently was not drafted. He married Mergie Williamson and they had four children as listed below:

Edward J. Ball was killed during World War II in Italy on March 16, 1944. He served with the U. S. 8th Army, 31st Field Artillery, Company B of the 52nd Quarter Master, Truck Battalion, and died of wounds sustained in the fighting.

Joseph Eugene, called "Gene," married Janette Ball and had one daughter Pam Thomas. He worked as a foreman for Satterfield Construction in Rankin County, and died in the Rankin General Hospital on July 22, 1986.

Jimmie Eva (1921-1982) was married three times; had at least one daughter, Ora Nell "Billie" (1939-2000); and at one point was charged with "Desertion of Minor Children." The outcome of the trial is unknown. Jimmie, whose last husband was Jimmie Dean Williams, died in Tupelo, Mississippi, on March 9, 1982, and is buried in Pontotoc, Mississippi. [Note: Interestingly, Jimmie Eva married Jimmie Dean!]

The other daughter was Mary Etta. No further information is available for her.

Mercer Ball, another son of Lewis and Mollie, was listed on the 1910 census as being 1½ years old, making his date of birth 1908. He died on December 26, 1919, in Jackson, Mississippi, at the age of eleven. He was buried in Mendenhall, Mississippi.

Mollie White Ball:

Mollie White Ball, the widow and second wife of Lewis Ball, died in the Jackson Infirmary in Jackson, Mississippi, on October 16, 1932. Apparently, she had been living with one of her children prior to her death. She was buried in the Macedonia Baptist Church cemetery near Mendenhall in Simpson County.

The Older Children of Lewis and Margaret Lou:

German Washington Ball:

Kin

On the 1910 census German Ball was living with his uncles Joe E. and Wallace Boggan on a farm in Mendenhall. He was described as a boarder/farmer, and he was twenty years old. He was listed as single, but he married Oba "Obie" Williamson the next year.

German and Obie moved to Louisiana where German applied for the draft for World War I. He was described as medium build and medium weight with black hair and light blue eyes. He was engaged in farming and worked for D. C. Parkinson. He had a wife and baby which apparently kept him out of the war.

By 1920 German and Obie had two sons, Avery and Clarence W. Ball, and in August of that year, a daughter, Audrey Mae, was born into the family.

In the 1930 census the family was still living in West Carroll Parish, Louisiana. They did not own property but rented a house, and the census said they had no radio! Clarence was twelve and Audrey was nine, but there was no mention of Avery who must have died sometime since the 1920 census.

In the 1940 census, German was 50 years old. He and Obie were still in West Carroll Parish and their son Clarence, who was twenty-two, was living with them.

There was no 1950 census available on the internet, but in 1962, German died. He had been sick a long time, although the cause of his illness is unknown. A funeral was held at the Coax Baptist Church in Baskin, Louisiana, and he was buried in the church cemetery.

Obie died on March 15, 1971, at age 78. Like German, she had also been ill a long time and died in the hospital. Her funeral was also held at the Coax Baptist Church with burial in the church cemetery.

Their son Clarence married Earline Tennyson on May 23, 1942, in Jefferson, Alabama. Clarence was 24 years old at the time of his marriage. He registered for the World War II draft and served in the African Theater in the U. S. Army Air Force. He was a sergeant and served as a supply clerk.

After the war Clarence was an auditor at Northeast Louisiana State College for a number of years and was eventually promoted to business manager. On April 7, 1969, he was driving and felt ill, so he pulled over to the side of the road. He suffered a fatal stroke. Although he lived in St. Francisville, his funeral and burial were held at the Coax Baptist Church in Baskin.

Daughter Aubrey Mae married Lawrence Edward Brand from Conroe, Texas, on May 8, 1938. Like his brother-in-law, Lawrence registered for the World War II draft where he is described as 5'6" tall and weighing 135 pounds. He had grey eyes, blonde hair, and a light complexion.

Aubrey and Lawrence had three sons, but Buddy Joe Brand died as an infant. The other sons were John Edward Brand and Douglas Brand.

On March 11, 2000, Lawrence died in Winnsboro, Louisiana, where they were living at the time. After his death, Aubrey moved to McComb, Mississippi, where she died on August 16, 2003, at age 83. Like the rest of her family, she is buried at the Coax Baptist Church in Baskin, Louisiana.

Georgia Ball Boone:

Lewis and Margaret Lou's daughter and the sister of German and Hattie Ball, Georgia married at age seventeen. She married John Greene Boone and they had a number of children:

Luther Ellis Boone was born on November 20, 1908, in Simpson County. He married Clemmie Junior Hall in Magee, and they had two daughters and two sons:

Dora Georgann Boone (born May 6, 1941) married Dan Lee Boyd, Sr. (born August 6, 1939). Their children were Dan Lee Boyd, Jr. (born June 18, 1960) and Martha Ann Boyd (born August 2, 1962);

Billy Gerald Boone (born January 4, 1943) married Barbara Sue McConnel (born October 2, 1945). They married on May 29, 1965, and were the parents of Christopher Gerald Boone (born August 3, 1970);

Bettie Lou Boone (born June 19, 1944) married McLoyn Lauarne Hardy (born October 15, 1943). They married on May 27, 1963, and had two children: Tanya Kathleen Hardy (born July 3, 1964) and Michelle Rene Hardy (born December 14, 1966);

Robert Mitchell Boone, Sr. (born September 3, 1948) married Claudia Ann Fisk. Their son was Robert Mitchell Boone, Jr. (born July 6, 1970).

John Calvin Boone was born on June 8, 1912, also in Simpson County. He married Katie Lavernia Runnel Hughes (previously married to W. A. Hughes, deceased). J. C. was a carpenter employed by the J. A. Jones Construction Company, and they were members of D'Lo Baptist Church. They had one daughter Mildred who married Charles E. McCallum. J. C. died on January 29, 1958, in Jackson at age 46. He was buried in the Sharon Cemetery in Coats, Mississippi. Mildred and Charles had six children:

> Charles Michael, born December 29, 1953;
> Janet Denise, born August 16, 1955; died March 25, 1963;
> Deborah Arlon, born September 6, 1963;
> Keith Rondell born May 12, 1965;
> Suzanne Jeanele, born December 31, 1966;
> James Stacy, burn March 4, 1970.

Leonard Exodus Boone was born on February 11, 1915, and died on April 29, 1991, at age 76. He married Mary Nell Ellis (born December 20, 1919). Leonard is buried at the Lakewood South Memorial Park in Jackson. Their son was Earl Lee Boone.

> Earl Lee Boone (born July 24, 1937), married 1) Bessie Lucile Jackson (born August 25, 1938), 2) Georgie Lucile McKenzie (born June 24, 1933). By his first wife he had four children: Cliff Earl (born September 13, 1955); Carolyn Lucile (born October 1, 1956); Karen Sue (born July 16, 1959); and John Edward (born October 31, 1960).

Eula Louise Boone was the first daughter born to Georgia and John, and she was born on May 11, 1919, in Rankin County, Mississippi. She married Bonnar Lee Thames (born September 6, 1904 and died October 29, 1961). They had two sons: James Truett Thames (born February 24, 1939) and Jimmy D. Thames (born April 4, 1940, married Betty Ruth Gardner on July 28,

1961). Louise died at age 62 on June 19, 1981, and is buried at the Pine Grove Baptist Church Cemetery in Magee, Mississippi.

Burley Robert Boone was born on July 30, 1921, in Rankin County. He married Edith Evolia McNeil (born on June 14, 1924) in May 1941, and they lived in Century, Florida. Burley died on August 29, 2003, and is buried in the Hollywood Cemetery in Flomaton, Escambia County, Florida.

> Burley's daughter was Ada Jonez Boone, born on October 9, 1943. She married William Frank Barren, Sr. (born in April 1938). They were married on November 9, 1960, and had two children: Willie Frankie Barron, Jr., (born October 15, 1961) and John Edward Barron (born on October 31, 1963).

> Burley's two sons were Richard Burland Boone (born February 28, 1947) who married Sandra Eleene Schueller (born December 25, 1942) and Robert Martin Boone was born on April 2, 1949, and married Shirley Ann Hathorne (born Jan 26, 1945).

Eunice O. Boone married William Allen McClain and they lived in Houston, Texas. He served in World War II which allowed both of them to be buried in the national cemetery in Houston, Texas. William died on April 20, 2012, and Eunice died on January 8, 2016, at age 91. They had three children:

> Judy Allen McClain (born March 26, 1946) married Dan Valton McKinley (born May 2, 1943) on August 31, 1968; Sherry Anne McClain (born August 10, 1948) married John Michael McSwain (born November 1, 1946) on October 26, 1968; and Sandra Lee McClain (born November 20, 1953).

Loretta Jane Boone was born on October 29, 1927. She married Hulon Harvey Cockrell, and they had three children:

> John Hulon Cockrell (born July 7, 1953);
> George Steven Cockrell (born November 11, 1952);
> Ouida Carol Cockrell Wilcher (born on November 25, 1954).

Loretta worked in a garment factory, and Hulon was employed by the Mississippi Industries for the Blind. They made their home in Magee, Mississippi. At age 63, Hulon Cockrell died, and on June 27, 2001, at age 73, Loretta died. Both are buried in Sharon Cemetery in Coats, Simpson County.

Bobby Martin Boone was born on December 24, 1929. He married Barbara McNeil (born June 25, 1932), and they lived in Canton, Mississippi. Bobby was a long-distance truck driver, and the father of two children:

> Brenda Bernice Boone (born October 22, 1953) married Winfred Larry Murphy (born May 8, 1943). Brenda and Winfred had four children: Timothy Russell Murphy Boone; Joseph Martin Murphy Boone, Jerry Leland Murphy Boone, Pamela Murphy Boone Huskey.

> Virginia Aileen Boone Sizer (born December 4, 1951) married Johnny Davis Thrach, Sr.

Bobby was a veteran of World War II, having served from August 8, 1944, until February 14, 1945. He died at age 85 on April 28, 2015, in Canton but was buried in the Natchez Trace Memorial Park in Madison, Mississippi.

The last child of Georgia and John Boone was Draughn Lee Boone who was born on December 11, 1933. He and his wife Linda had three daughters: Glenda, Cindy, and Wanda. He lived in Pearl, Mississippi, for thirty-six years and was a heavy-duty parts salesman for Standard GMC, Yellow Freight, and others. He died on October 5, 2005, of liver cancer and was buried in the Floral Hills Memory Garden in Pearl.

[Source for the above information: Papers of Nora Beatrice Brown Byrd]

Georgia's husband was a farmer, and with a house full of children, Georgia spent her time being a wife, mother, and housekeeper. Her husband, John, registered for the draft for World War I, and he was described as tall and slender with black hair and blue eyes. He was 38 years old at the time.

Through the years the family lived in a number of towns in Mississippi: In Simpson County; Cato, Puckett, and Brandon in Rankin County; and in Smith County. John lived to be eighty years old and died on September 13, 1960. He was buried in Magee at the Siloam Baptist Church cemetery.

Georgia was ninety-two when she died on May 13, 1983. She had been living in Brandon, probably in or near the home of one of her children. Her funeral service was held at 4:00 p.m. on Saturday of that week in the Mims Mitchell Funeral Home Chapel with burial in Siloam Cemetery in Simpson County. She was survived by sons Luther, Leonard, Burley, Bobby, and Lee; and daughters Eunice and Loretta. Her half-brother, Jewell Ball, of Jackson also survived her, as did 25 grandchildren, 44 great-grandchildren and seven great-great-grandchildren!

Hattie Jane Ball Brown:

Hattie Jane Ball lived a sad life, but as her daughter Nora described her, "she was sweet." Hattie was only four when her mother died, and her father remarried. Soon Hattie was surrounded with younger siblings and half-siblings. Her brother German was only three, and her sister Georgia was one. There were half-siblings: Jewell, born three years later; Dan born in another two years; and Byron, born the next year. Being the oldest daughter, Hattie had to help in the care of all these little children.

For whatever reason, the older children (Hattie, German, and Georgia) went to live with their maternal grandparents, Alex and Nancy Boggan, who lived nearby in Simpson County. In the 1900 census Hattie was twelve years old, German was ten, and Georgia was nine. Their mother's sister, Lizzie Boggan, also lived in the home.

The children worked on the farm and helped with the housework. They attended school for a while and were members of Macedonia Baptist Church. Their grandfather died in 1909, but their grandmother lived another ten years until 1919.

In 1907 Hattie married George Matthew Brown who also grew up in Simpson County. How they met or how long they had known each other is unknown, but they established a home in Weathersby near their relatives. Soon their children were born:

Sarah Lessie Brown was born on November 21, 1908;
Mary Letha Brown was born on August 22, 1910;
Nora Beatrice was born on July 6, 1912;
John Grady Brown was born on February 28, 1914.

Hattie's father, Lewis Ball, died prior to the 1910 census, which might have brought more sadness into her young life.

And then more sadness came when her husband, George Brown, died of tuberculosis on February 9, 1917, just three years after the last child was born. George had been a 32nd Degree Mason which enabled Hattie and the children to move into the Masonic Widows and Orphans Home in Meridian, Mississippi. Since George and Hattie had not bought a house in Weathersby, this was a good alternative.

The girls were placed in the Orphans Home, Grady was sent to the Boy's Farm (owned by the Home) at some point, and Hattie got a job in the Home's laundry so she could be near her children.

Alas, Lessie developed tuberculosis like her father, and she was not allowed to live in the Home. Hattie took care of her as best as she could, but by the age of thirteen, Lessie died. She was buried next door to the Home in the Magnolia Cemetery, Meridian.

Hattie lived with various relatives for short periods, and from time to time she rented a house so the children could live with her during the summers when school was not in session. Her granddaughter, Joy Byrd Rich, tells the story of one incident which happened during one of these visits.

> The children had been taught to avoid using the word "bull." One day Hattie left the children at home alone, and while she was gone, a big, black bull came up to the fence on the property. The children were so excited and enjoyed talking to the bull over the fence.
>
> When Hattie returned, the children excitedly told her that a big, black "gentleman" had come up to the fence. He was so friendly, and they talked to him a long time! Hattie was horrified that a person had been in their back yard while she was away and had been talking to her children, not realizing the "gentleman" was merely a bull!

Sadly, Hattie could not be with the children during their various childhood illnesses, and often the children were left unattended at the Orphans Home when it was suspected that they were contagious.

In the 1930s Hattie married Daniel C. Whitlock who was from the Meridian area and was employed in the soft-drink industry. As a young man of 26, Daniel was single and lived with his parents on a farm in Tunnel Hill, Mississippi; and later, as noted on the World War I draft card, he was still living in Lauderdale County.

How and where Hattie met Daniel is unknown, but after their marriage they moved to Smith County. Letha and Grady moved into the home with them, but, apparently, Nora was in college and did not live in the Whitlock home.

Sadly, Hattie soon realized she had made a serious mistake. She left Daniel and, as far as the family was aware, kept the married name of Brown for the rest of her life. [However, in 1942 when Grady enlisted in the army, his mother was identified as "Hattie G. [sic] Whitlock."] There has been no record of an official divorce or annulment found.

On the 1940 census Hattie and Grady were living together in Jackson. She was 51 years old in 1939 and she (or Grady) had rented a house. Family lore says that when Grady graduated from high school, his mother told him to provide her with a home. Perhaps this was the home he provided.

Grady was drafted in 1942, and it is not known where Hattie lived while he was gone. Grady married Dorothy "Dot" Diffenderfer in 1943, and from that time on, Hattie lived with them. She applied for Social Security benefits after 1936.

Dot described her mother-in-law as opinionated and at times hard to take, but Grady was sweet to his mother and never asked her to keep her opinions to herself.

On July 20, 1950, Hattie Jane Ball Brown (Whitlock) died. She was buried in the Macedonia Baptist Church cemetery in Weathersby (near Mendenhall), Mississippi, beside George Matthew Brown.

Children of Hattie Ball Brown:

1. Sarah Lessie Ball was born on August 22, 1908, in Weathersby, Simpson County. She died of tuberculosis on September 19, 1922, and is buried in the Magnolia Cemetery, Meridian, Mississippi.

2. Mary Letha Brown was born on August 22, 1910, in Weathersby. She married Felix Daughtry Wilder (1901-1981). Letha died of tuberculosis on March 2, 1948, and is buried in the Magnolia Cemetery adjacent to the Widows and Orphans Home in Meridian.

3. Nora Beatrice Brown was born on July 6, 1912, in Weathersby. She married Edward Leavell Byrd (1912-2004), and was the mother of three children: Edward Leavell, Byrd, Jr., Hersey Davis Byrd, and Beatrice Joy Byrd Rich. After a bout with cancer, Nora died on June 25, 1998, in Edgewood, Kentucky, where she and Edward had retired. She was buried in Mount Hope Cemetery, Florence, South Carolina. [More information is available on Nora Brown Byrd in the companion book, *Oaks of Righteousness,* by this author.]

4. John Grady Brown was born on February 28, 1914, served in the U. S Army during World War II, and married Dorothy Lucille Diffenderfer on November 25, 1943. He was the father of Joyce Marie Brown Bradshaw and George Raleigh Brown. Grady died of cancer on December 18, 1978, and was buried in the Lakewood South Memorial Park in Jackson.

The link between the Ball family and the Byrd family rests with Hattie Jane Ball and through her daughter, Nora Brown Byrd, who married Edward Leavell Byrd. They were the parents of Hersey Davis Byrd.

Sources:
John H. Lang: *History of Harrison County Mississippi,* Internet Information.
Findadgrave.com/memorial/...
Ancestry.com
MyHeritage.com
FamilySearch.com
Personal Papers of Nora Brown Byrd.
Personal Conversations with Joy Byrd Rich, H. Davis Byrd, and other family members.
On-Site Visits and Observations.

Kay Byrd

THE BETHEA FAMILY

How does the Bethea Family relate to the Byrd Family? It is assumed that Hopey Rogers, the wife of Shadrack Meshack Abednego Rogers, was Hopey Bethea prior to her marriage; however, there is NO documentation to confirm her last name. Hopey married Shadrack Rogers; their granddaughter Malissa Rogers married John King Byrd, and his grandson was Edward Leavell Byrd, the father of Hersey Davis Byrd.

Some researchers have suggested that Hopey was from the Berthier family, but there is little or no information available on the internet for this family. There is also speculation that her maiden name could have been Manning, or Tatum, or Reddick. Bethea seems likely for the following reasons.

There were several land-purchase records in Dillon County and Marion County, South Carolina, for Shadrack Rogers, and sometimes for Shadrack and Hopey Rogers. Shadrack was apparently from this region although his actual place of birth and lineage is also unclear. In this same area are many Bethea families. It seems likely that Shadrack would have chosen a Bethea girl to be his bride since he was buying land among the Bethea family members.

One of Hopey's grandsons was named Bethea. Could this have been a reference to Hopey's family?

[Note: A visit to the old Bethea home place in Dillon, South Carolina, revealed a lovely, old, two-story home known as "Woodlawn." It was built c. 1785 by Sarah Rogers Manning and Mealy (Melea) Manning. Although the home has been in the Bethea family for decades, it is currently in need of extensive repair and was recently for sale.]

The Bethea family has kept extensive records on their ancestors and there is an actual "Bethea Family Genealogy Website." It seems the family originated in France and were possibly Huguenots, since they were Protestants. The family traces its ancestors to John Bethea, who left France, fled to England, and then emigrated to America around 1700. He was offered Indian land "on the James River for homesteading in Virginia," but preferred to settle "elsewhere in Virginia and...along Chesapeake Bay and Albemarle Sound to the South, near the old community of Suffolk, Va."

Harlee's Kinfolks History, Volume III, identifies John Bethea as "English" John Bethea who had at least two sons. English John deeded his land in what was then Gates County, North Carolina, to his son Tristam with the provision that he, English John Bethea, be allowed to live on the land and in his home until his death. Tristam and his children continued to live in this area and expanded along the Cape Fear River. This family became known as the "Marlborough Bethea branch and he [Tristam] raised a large family with four sons and five daughters."

The other son, John, was identified as "Virginia" John, and he and his children settled in the area which became Dillon County, South Carolina. John "married Sarah Darby and was the father of four children. Two sons and at least two daughters, who married into the Rogers family, and moved to Dillon County, South Carolina."

The two brothers [children of Virginia John] eventually became neighbors in the Dillon area and were given new nicknames: "Sweatswamp William" Bethea and "Buckswamp John" Bethea. These nicknames reflected the creeks on which their lands were located. The Sweat Swamp actually "flowed into the Little Pee Dee River, along which many Betheas resided by 1800."

"By 1800, when the United States of America was well established, and President Thomas Jefferson was purchasing new lands in the Western frontier (the Louisiana Purchase), some of the Bethea descendants set out by horse and wagon to Georgia, to Alabama, to Mississippi, and then crossing the great Mississippi River, to Arkansas, to Texas and beyond, seeking homestead lands in the new U. S. frontier." [Information from the Bethea Family website]

An internet note says that "Hopey Bethea was the youngest child of John Bethea/Bathey also known as 'Virginia John' by descendants to distinguish him from his father, "English" John. Her mother was reportedly Sarah Darby Bishop. Her siblings were: William Bethea [aka "Sweatswamp William"] who married Sarah Goodman; Mary [who married William Stackhouse]; John [aka "Buckswamp John"] who married Absala Parker; and Anna [who married Lot Rogers]. I have that she was born 1762 in Marion County (I think it was the Cheraw District at that time), SC, married Shadrack Rogers and died 1838 in Covington, Mississippi. Burial at the Meshack Rogers Cemetery in Covington County, SC."

At any rate there is documented evidence that Shadrack Rogers' wife was named Hopey. They were probably married in South Carolina prior to 1790. They lived in the northeastern part of South Carolina, amassed a great many acres of land, which they then sold and moved further inland to the old Sumter District of South Carolina around 1800. There, more land was purchased and then sold by 1818.

[Note: It is interesting that Shadrack and Hopey's first child was named Timothy, which is presumably the name of Shadrack's father. Their second child was named Reddick, the name of the minister who performed their wedding, presumably. However, generally in Southern families of old, the second child bears the name of the mother's family. Could Hopey's father have been a Reddick?

Son Timothy named his son, Whitten Bethea Rogers. Was Bethea the maiden name of his mother, Hopey?]

Apparently, Hopey had a strong personality, or Shadrack had other sufficient reasons to include her on many of his land negotiations. It was somewhat unusual to have the wife's name and signature on land purchases and sales, but Hopey's name appears on a number of Shadrack's South Carolina dealings.

All eight of their children were born in South Carolina, and with their children and their children's families, they formed a caravan and headed west to Mississippi. They settled in what is now Covington County, Mississippi, along the banks of what was to be named "Rogers Creek."

The link between the Bethea Family and the Byrd Family lies with Hopey. Their grandson Josiah married Kisiah Duckworth, and Josiah and Kisiah's grandson was James Edward Byrd, the father of Edward Leavell Byrd. Edward Byrd was Hersey Davis Byrd's father.

Kin

www.betheafamily.org;
www.Myheritage.com/names/hope.rodgers;
www.ancestry.co.uk/boards/surnames.bethea/11.90.1.1.1.1.1/mb.ashx;
www.ancestry.com/boards/surnames.bethea/11.90/mb.ashx;
Ancestral Key to the Pee Dee by Mary Belle Manning Bethea (Columbia, SC: R. L. Bryan Company, 1978);
History of Marion County by W. W. Sellers (Greenville, SC: Southern Historical Press, 1902)
Kinfolks, Volume III, by Willian Curry Harllee (New Orleans: Searcy & Pfaff, Ltd., 1937)

Kay Byrd

THE BOGGAN FAMILY

How does the Boggan family relate to the Byrd family?

Margaret Lou Boggan married Lewis Ball. Their daughter, Hattie Jane Ball, had a daughter named Nora Beatrice Brown, who married Edward Leavell Byrd, and was the mother of Hersey Davis Byrd.

The Boggan story begins with **John Boggan,** who was born after 1648 in Ireland. He married Guinevere Madison, and they were the parents of at least one son, Walter Boggan. John died after 1703 in Ireland.

Walter Boggan was born in 1694 in the little village of Castlefinn in County Donegal, Ulster, Ireland. He was a prominent member of Irish royalty and was known as Sir Walter Boggan. He married Lydia O'Rorie Moore whose family was wealthy. [Note: The O'Rorie Moore family left Ireland and moved to Barbados and later settled in Charleston, South Carolina.] As a result of their marriage, Sir Walter acquired a large estate and built a castle on his lands.

Sir Walter was the father of Mary Jane Wade (1723), Patrick Henry Boggan (1725), Benjamin Boggan (1727), Walter Howard Boggan (1733), **James Boggan, Sr.** (1740), William Boggan (1744), and Henry Boggan (1748).

[Note: When we visited Castlefinn several years ago, we discovered that the castle had been destroyed and the rocks from the castle had been used to build a small bridge over the stream that runs alongside the village of Castlefinn. There are no longer any Boggans in Castlefinn, the last remaining Boggan having left several months prior to our visit.]

Sir Walter died on April 24, 1756 or 1760 in Castlefinn. The exact year of his death is uncertain.
[Source: geni.com/people/Sir-Walter-Boggan/6000000000823112134]

Children of Sir Walter Boggan:

When Sir Walter Boggan died, his sons Patrick, James, and Benjamin and his daughter Jane traveled to America. They were well educated and "could write their names on the many documents that they signed, rather than making their Mark X, much used for a signature in those days."
[Source: *The Boggan Family* compiled by Frances Henrietta Bingham Krechel and found on Ancestry.com]

Kin

Why did the Irish leave Ireland? In his book, *North Carolina-Highlanders, Scotch, Irish and Germans*, Mr. Lefler said:

> The ship's captains, agents of land companies and others were interested in procuring indentured servants for the colonial labor market. Of the 3,200 shipped to America in 1725-28, …only one in ten could pay for his own passage. A writer in an Irish magazine calculated that from 3,000 to 6,000 annually emigrated in the years 1725-1768. Naval records reveal that 5,835 'Irish servants' landed at Annapolis, Maryland, in the years 1745-1775.

In *The Boggan Family* story, Mrs. Krechel speculated that the Boggan siblings were "swept along in this tide, but if of Irish Nobility, [they] were the one in ten that could pay."

"They landed at one of the Northern ports, possibly New York, [Annapolis], or Philadelphia, as a great majority of the earlier settlers in this nation did." They traveled "through Maryland and Virginia, in which states they tarried for a while, thence to South Carolina." About the year 1765, they came to the area later named Anson County, North Carolina.

Apparently, Benjamin chose to live in Virginia and settled in the old Frederick County, an area so large that it encompasses five present-day West Virginia counties and three Virginia counties. Benjamin Boggan is listed in the Revolutionary War records as serving Virginia in the war and was promoted from private to sergeant to corporal.

It is possible that he married Catherine Lewis in Frederick County on June 12, 1788. This couple had a son whom they named Benjamin Lewis Boggan (1795-1870). It is also possible that this family later moved to Alabama, although definitive information has not been located.
[Source: Alabama, Surname Files Expanded, 102-1981]

Another possible relative, William Boggan, Sr., was listed on the Chester County, Pennsylvania, tax rolls as early as 1740. His relationship to Sir Walter's children is unknown, and, interestingly, he signed his documents with his Mark X. William Boggan, Sr., and William Boggan, Jr. were later found in records of Anson County, North Carolina, meaning they had also traveled "…south where the land is cheap," a current land agent appeal. A genealogist wrote that the Boggan siblings were "Scotch Presbyterian and brought with them a book, *Confession of Faith of the Presbyterian*

Church." Later generations joined the Methodist Church, and many were Episcopalians.
[Source: Ancestry.com "The Boggan Family"]

Of the two brothers, Patrick and James, Patrick was the colorful one. Legend has it that Patrick was a "very robust and stout man...very agile and powerful man physically and...he could run and jump over a covered wagon body placed on the ground." [*The Boggan Family*]

DAR records have the following information about Patrick Boggan:

> In the year 1768 an outbreak on the part of Anson County seems to have been the first open resistance to oppressions on the part of the crown. Even at this date it was said that taxation and representation should always be associated. Patrick Boggan was one of the strongest who formed themselves into a company who would fight unto the death for their rights.

[Note: Apparently, this act of aggression was seen as the first resistance to the Crown in the Colonies, which enabled North Carolina to identify itself as "First in Freedom."]

Patrick was a Revolutionary War hero and was affectionately called "Cap'n Paddy" or an "adventuresome Irishman." Mary Medley in her book, *History of Anson County, North Carolina 1750-1976,* describes Patrick as an "athletic, sandy-haired courageous fighter." He was Captain of Militia and received his commission from General Nathanael Green. He served in Colonel Thomas Wade's "Minute Men" of the Salisbury District as captain of a company of Minute Men.

[The designations of minutemen and militia are confusing, but Mary Medley explained the military divisions by quoting Archibald Henderson:

> The military organization set up in 1775-76 comprised three general divisions. The Militia, The Minutemen, and the Continentals, or Regulars. The designation Minutemen was not continued officially after 1776...]

Patrick had a fierce hatred of Tories. "There is a tradition that when he was spending one night at home, three Tories, armed to the teeth, surrounded his house and demanded that he surrender. They intended to kill him. He hid his wife's flax knife in his coat, went out meekly among the three Tories, made an attack on them, and killed all three with the flax knife before they could recover from their surprise." [*The Boggan Family*]

Patrick amassed a large holding of lands in present-day Anson County, North Carolina, and parts of upper South Carolina. Another story was told regarding Patrick's generosity. Colonel Thomas Wade was Patrick's friend and his brother-in-law. Patrick told Wade to help himself to [Patrick's] land, and Wade did just that. "...he took all of 'Newtown', sold lots and named it Wadesboro. The recorded deed does not say it was a deed of gift."

> The town of Wadesboro dates back to 1783 when it was founded by Capt. Patrick Boggan and Col. Thomas Wade, famous Revolutionary War patriots.
>
> A settlement had grown along the banks of the Pee Dee River, but a more centralized location was needed for the county seat. The new site was found, and seventy acres of land were purchased by Patrick Boggan. Streets were laid out and named for Revolutionary War notables including Generals George Washington, Nathaniel Greene, Daniel Morgan and Griffith Rutherford; Colonels Thomas Wade and William Washington; and Governors Richard Caswell and Alexander Martin. The town was first called New Town, later changed to Wadesborough and then Wadesboro...
>
> The oldest house in Wadesboro is the Boggan-Hammond House on East Wade Street. Built by Capt. Patrick Boggan for his daughter, Nellie, wife of William Hammond, it is now a historical museum maintained by the Anson County Historical Society. [Source: **townofwadesboro.org/history-of-wadesboro.html**]

Patrick lived in the Boggan-Hammond house with his daughter Nellie in the final years of his life. "Capt. Paddy...had gone out into the woods near the cemetery to feed his hogs and was found dead with a basket of corn on his arm." The date of his death and the location of his grave are unknown.

Patrick's sister, Jane Boggan, married Thomas Wade, the Revolutionary War hero and patriot. He was a civic leader during and after the "War of the Revolution" and continued to be instrumental in local affairs until his death in 1786.

James Boggan, Sr.

Patrick and Jane's brother, James Boggan, was born on March 17, 1740, in Castlefinn, Ireland, and married Jennie (or Jeannie) in 1759. They had fourteen children:

Margaret, 1760;
James, 1762, married Judette Lowry;
John, born June 9, 1763 and died June 21, 1818;
Jane, 1765;
Mary, 1767;
William, 1768;
Solomon, 1770;
Joseph, born June 27, 1772 and died in June 1871;
Jennie, 1774;
Jesse, 1776;
Jonathan, 1779;
Charles, 1780, married Sarah Grizzard, moved to Monroe
   County, Mississippi;
Thomas, 1782;
Abner, born May 11, 1788.

James "signed many documents, was a Justice of the Peace and has been established as a Patriot with the Daughters of the American Revolution since 1972. He was the executor of Thomas Wade's will. [Source: members.aol.com/InmanGA/family.mask.]

Like his brother, James was a well-respected citizen of Wadesboro. He acquired a large holding of property and supported the "Regulators" [as the soldiers from Anson County were called] in the Revolutionary War. He served as an officer in the War and was the father of Major James Boggan, another local Revolutionary War hero.

Several of James' adult children moved westward, settling in Alabama and Mississippi. Jesse and Joseph moved to Simpson County, Mississippi; Charles moved to Monroe County, Mississippi; and Jonathan moved to Butler County, Alabama.

Both James and his wife Jennie died in Anson County, but their dates of death and location of their graves are unknown, although they are supposedly buried somewhere in the Eastview Cemetery in Wadesboro.

Kin

[Source: A personal visit at the Anson County Historical Society]

[NOTE: There is a lovely old home in Wadesboro which was used as a funeral home for many years. This home was built by James Boggan's grandson, Norfleet Boggan, and is another reminder of the impact of the Boggan family in Anson County, North Carolina.]

There is information about James Boggan in the early years of Simpson County, Mississippi. In *Early Living* by Bee King, James Boggan was listed as one of "The first settlers along Silver Creek." Also, a history of Simpson County says, "Shortly after the county was organized, an act of the legislature designed [sic] Daniel McCaskell, James B. Satterfield, William Herring, *James Boggan*, Peter Stubbs and Jacob Carr as a committee to locate a county seat within three miles of the center of the county." The site this committee selected was in the Westville area which was also the location of later Boggan lands. All public records were burned in a courthouse fire in 1872, "a loss that is still felt by the many families who would treasure information concerning their ancestors."

[Source: http://ourworld.cs.com/uptondavid/simpsonfolk/eliving.htm; and http://home.earthlink.net/~rooo22/simpson1.htm which also notes: Reprinted from 'Simpson County Sesquicentennial Historical Booklet 1974']

It is unlikely that James Boggan, Sr., moved to Mississippi due to his age, but there is a strong possibility that his son, Major James Boggan, might have moved westward. As an American patriot in the Revolutionary War, he could have been granted land in the Mississippi territory.

Jesse Boggan

One of the sons of James and Jennie Boggan moved west to Simpson County. Jesse Boggan, who was born on December 12, 1776, married Mary "Polly" Edwards, who was born about 1792. They were the parents of seven children:

> Margaret Boggan was born on April 6, 1822, in Anson County, North Carolina, and died on June 1, 1880, in Mississippi. She married William "Billy" D. King, and they had a number of children. Margaret's Findagrave website lists names of six children: Lewis Uriah, Elias, William Denis, Maggie, John Walter, and Nancy Jane. Other names appearing on the various census records are Needham, Elizar, and Sara.

Samuel Pleasant Boggan, a Confederate soldier, was born in 1826 in North Carolina before the family moved west. He married Matilda Butler (1832) and was the father of at least four children: William, Jesse, Mary, and Eliza. Pleasant enlisted in Company G of the Mississippi 8th Infantry on September 15, 1863, and later served in Company H as a private. Pleasant died on April 10, 1893, at age 67 and was buried in the Boggan Cemetery in Simpson County, Mississippi.

Eliza Boggan was the oldest daughter of Jesse and Polly Edwards. She was born on January 24, 1825 and married James A. Smith. They had four daughters and two sons, but Eliza along with daughters Harriet and Priscilla, died in a tragic house fire on March 17, 1851. She was also buried in the Boggan Cemetery.

Alexander B. Boggan was born in Anson County, North Carolina, on March 29, 1829. [More information on this direct ancestor follows this listing of his siblings.]

Jesse James Boggan was born in Simpson County, Mississippi, on December 22, 1832. Although he carried the name of a famous outlaw, Jesse was named for his father and grandfather. His wife was Amanda Jane Farmer and they had nine children: Thomas Jefferson, Mary Ann, William Pink, Altamyrah Elizabeth, Amanda Jane, Margarett Eliza, Louvenia, Samuel Noah, and Nathaniel Berry. Jesse also served in the Civil War. He enlisted in Company H, Mississippi 6th Infantry and rose to the rank of sergeant. Unfortunately, he was captured by Union forces and was held as a Prisoner of War in the Military Prison in Louisville, Kentucky. Jesse outlived the war and died on May 25, 1897, in Simpson County. He is buried in the Boggan Cemetery.

Mary Boggan was born on October 1, 1834, and died seventy years later on October 10, 1904. She married Solomon Walker, and they were the parents of six sons: George W. Walker, Asa Laurin Walker, J. Hugh Walker, J. B. Walker, Solomon Frank Walker, and Robert E. Lee Walker. Mary's husband was in Company H of the 6th Mississippi Infantry during the Civil War. He was a corporal.

Harriet Boggan was born in 1836 and married Isom McLendon. They had at least three children as shown on the 1860 census: Rebecca, Needham, and Scott. A schoolteacher, John M Murray, lived in their home.

Jesse and Polly made their home in Simpson County as did most of their children. Jesse died on March 27, 1838, and Polly died twenty years later on January 2, 1858. They were buried on family property in what was to become known as the Boggan Cemetery.

Alexander B. Boggan

As previously mentioned, Alex Boggan was born in Anson County, North Carolina, on December 12, 1776. He married a North Carolina girl named Nancy Jane McLendon, and they caught the fervor to move west where land was plentiful and cheap. They chose to make their home in what is now a ghost town called Westville, Mississippi. It was located in the southern part of Simpson County and offered red and yellow sandy loam soil. It was very hilly and not too good for large-scale farming, but it had masses of long-leaf pines and pleasant grasses. The nearby Strong River did offer dark, sandy loam and was excellent for producing corn, cotton, and hay.
[Source: books.google.com: *Geological and Mineral Resources of Mississippi*]

Shortly before their first child was born, Alex enlisted as a private in the Confederate army. He went to Grenada, Mississippi, and enlisted in the Mississippi 6th Regiment Infantry, Company H. He was made a sergeant sometime before the end of the war, and apparently was home from time to time since some of the children were born during the war.

Alex and Nancy Jane had eight children, all of whom were born in Simpson County and remained in this general area of Mississippi.

Louis Alexander Boggan was born on September 10, 1861, and married Laura Ella Clark. They had seven children:

Mary Maggie Boggan Pattie (1885-1970);
Pearlie Elizabeth Boggan Brown (1887-1964);
William "Willie" Jessie Boggan (1889-1971);
Washington "Wash" Alexander Boggan (1891-1959);
Beulah Jane Boggan Tarver Holyfield (1893-1986);

Clara Sarah Mandy Boggan (1897-1898);
Jasper Wayne Boggan.

In his obituary, Louis was described as an early pioneer of
Simpson County and a member of Macedonia Baptist Church. He
was buried in the church cemetery following his death on July
17, 1941.

Virginia Boggan Cruse and her parents knew these people personally. In
her genealogical book, *The Clark Family*, she shares some interesting
insights into the lives of the children of Louis A. Boggan, who was her
great-great grandfather.

"Beulah [Jane Boggan Holyfield] is remembered for the beautiful
handmade quilts, pillow slips, aprons, crocheted bedspreads,
tablecloths, and doilies that she made and so generously gave
to her nieces and nephews...

"After high school she got her teacher's certificate and became
principal of the small school known as Boggan School...Later she
took a teaching job at Enterprise, Louisiana, where she met and
married Bruce Tarver. They had two children, both of them
stillborn. Then her husband died, and she no longer wanted to
live in Louisiana, so she returned to Mississippi. Later she
married Hugh Holyfield. Then Beulah offered her home and
small service station in Grayson, Louisiana, to her brother,
Wayne, for just a fraction of what she had in it. He took the offer
and moved his family to Grayson where he resided until his
divorce in 1944.

"Beulah worked diligently to restore the Boggan Cemetery where
so many of her ancestors were buried..."

Wash Boggan had a daughter named Valeria who married
George Russell Sherman. "They had met one day when Valeria
and a friend were walking down the street in Mendenhall. When
the girls innocently (or not so innocently) waved at two good-
looking servicemen, the boys immediately turned their car
around, came back and 'picked them up.' This started their
courtship and a marriage that lasted over 61 years.

Kin

"Valeria and Sherman started a small country grocery store and service station, as well as farmed a large tract of land. They built large chicken houses and later started raising hogs for the market. They worked tirelessly. Sherman's mother came to live with them in her late life and they took care of her for many years. They also reared Sherman's nephew Vic Dickerson treating him just as they did their own children...Later when they gave up their store, Valeria went to work for a bank in Mendenhall. As the farm grew, Rusty [their son] joined Sherman in the family operations."

Valeria Boggan and George Sherman had two children, one of whom was Janice Faye Sherman. "Janice is a Children's Orthodontic Doctor. She had a glorious future in the work that she loved and had worked so hard to achieve. In her early 30s she was diagnosed with the debilitating illness called MS [Multiple Sclerosis]. This ended her career and started her on a life of ups and downs with her health. She has fought the battle relentlessly, and to a great degree, has lived a life of community service and faithfulness to her God." [Virginia Cruse]

Virginia Louise Boggan was the daughter of Jasper Wayne Boggan and Linna Beatrice Sanford Boggan. She was born on July 21, 1927, in rural Mendenhall "on what is known as Boggan Ridge even to this day. At that time there were Boggans on every ridge in Simpson County. She loved being close to her relatives both Boggans and Sanfords."

Her family moved to Grayson, Louisiana, where she graduated as Valedictorian of the Grayson High school. She met her husband, Benny Ray Cruse in high school and enjoyed going to "movies, which was the only past-time for young couples in Grayson."

Their first home was in Olla, Louisiana, where their first son, Dana Ray Cruse, was born. Their second son, Chuck, was born in Columbia, and they soon built a building supply business. They retired in 1982.

"Jasper Wayne Boggan, Jr., called Jay, was the grandson of Louis A. Boggan. He married Floye Pylant and they had a son named Raymond Jay Boggan who was a "happy and sensitive child and a very caring and benevolent man. He belonged to a motorcycle club that did many good deeds for needy people and for his community. Raymond Jay was killed by a murderer who served 21 years in the State Penitentiary at Angola, Louisiana, for the crime." Raymond died on June 29, 1986 in West Monroe, Louisiana.

Jay's other children were Jeffery Lee Boggan, Julia Lynn Boggan, and Joel Boggan. After the death of his first wife in 1992, Jay married Eva Neal. Both Jay and Eva died in West Monroe. [Source: Cruse, *The Clark Family*]

Mary Adline Boggan was the first daughter born to Alex and Nancy Jane Boggan and a sister to Louis A. Boggan. She was born on September 9, 1863, in the midst of the Civil War. At age 23 she married Jim B. Conner and began having many children: Ruth, Alex D., James, Jearl, Joseph "Joe", Sarah, and Mary. Jim died sometime before 1910 but the children stayed on the farm and helped manage it along with Mary. They owned their farm, mortgage free. Mary died on June 21, 1947, and is buried in the Macedonia Baptist Church Cemetery in Weathersby.

Margaret "Lou" Boggan was born just after the end of the Civil War on April 22, 1866. She was named for her aunt, Margaret Boggan, sister of her father. Lou married Lewis (or Louis) B. Ball on July 28, 1887, and they had three children: **Hattie Jane Ball**, German Washington Ball, and Georgia Ball. On June 16, 1892, when the older daughter, Hattie, was only four years old, Lou died. The cause of her death and where she is buried are unknown. [More on this family can be found in the Ball Family and the Brown Family chapters of this book.]

Two years after Lou's birth, another son was born into the family, William Jessie Boggan. He was born on November 2, 1868, and married three times. His first wife was Louisa Magdorah "Maggie" Clark. Her sister Ella Clark married William's brother, Louis A. Boggan, thereby making their children double cousins! They had three children: Martha "Marthy" Lenora (1891-1913); Alexander (1893-1969); and Lou Emma (1895-1944). Then Maggie died on March 4, 1987, and was buried in the Macedonia Baptist Church Cemetery.

Marthy, who was born on January 11, 1891, and died on March 22, 1913, married a Mr. Smith. She was buried in the Macedonia

Baptist Church Cemetery in Weathersby. No further information is available for her.

William Jessie's first son, Alex Louis Boggan, was born on January 29, 1895, and lived in Simpson County his whole life. He married Ora Effie Jones and they had three daughters: Margaret Nell, Tommie Fay, and Laura Lurene. They also raised an orphaned niece, Merl (or Myrl) Coleman. Their son was Dewey Emmitt Boggan. Alex died on March 13, 1969, and was also buried in the Macedonia Baptist Church Cemetery.

Lastly, Lou Emma married Abner Williamson. Emma was born in 1895 and died in 1930. They had one daughter Arlee Williamson, born in 1920 in Simpson County. Arlee married Cordas Burlian Walker and their two children were Cletus and Ella Lee.

William's second wife and the mother of eight more children was Laura Elizabeth Gardner from Copiah County. These children were:

1. Johnnie Louis Boggan (1898-1976) married twice in 1923. First, he married Bertie Jones (1902 - 1919) and after her death, he married Belle May (21 Mar 1903 - 05 May 1991) several months later. Bertie's obituary says: "As the sun was sinking low in the Western horizon, the death angel visited the home of J. L. Boggan on December 22, 1919, and took from him his dear bride of only thirteen months, she was ill only two days... She leaves...a little babe...She was loved by all who knew her for she had a smile and a kind word for all."

2. Louisa Nancie (1899-1978) married Henry Stephenson Williamson and they had a number of children: Frank, Ruby, Martha Etta, Nina Lou, Louise, Edna May, W. H. Larry, and Oliver Franklin. They lived in Simpson County all their lives and were members of Macedonia Baptist Church;

3. Lillie Belle Boggan (1902-1989) married Earnest Solomon Welch first and then married Estes Thomas Blair about 1962;

4. Janie Lee Boggan (1904-1993) married James Ethod Meadows. They had at least four children: Katherine Faye Meadows Jones, James Earl Meadows, Richard A. Meadows, and

Luther Otis Meadows. James and his mother, Janie, were both killed in an automobile accident on Highway 49 south of Mendenhall, where his father had died preciously.

5. William Estes (1906-1977) married Ruby Smith. William was the Superintendent of Education of Franklin County, Mississippi, schools. He and his wife lived in Bude, Mississippi. Ruby was a schoolteacher for nearly fifty years. She was affectionately known in Franklin County as "Mrs. Boggan" and, according to her obituary, "she was a very special lady, making each of her students feel special in her love and gentle attention toward each of them;"

6. Theodore Luther Boggan (1908-1998) married Julia "Junie" Lucinda Coleman, and they had three children: Luther, Laurene, and Doris. In his obituary he was described as a "Simpson County native. He was a past president of the Simpson County Farm Bureau and former district commissioner of Soil and Water Conservation. He was commissioner of State Soil and Water Conservation in 1997. He was a member of Simpson Economic Development in Simpson County, the Simpson Historical Society and the Simpson County School Board. He was inducted into the Mississippi Agricultural Museum Hall of Fame and was a member of Woodsmen of the World. He served on the Simpson County Baptist Association and was Sunday school director and a deacon at Macedonia Baptist Church. 'He was involved in every aspect of the community,' said son-in-law Ray Broadus of Mendenhall [Doris' husband]. If someone needed help, he was a person you could call on.'"

7. Milford Thomas Boggan (1911-1987) first married Ruby Lee Evans who was the mother of Thomas F. Boggan and Peggy Ann Boggan. Then he married Lucille L. [Unknown] who was the mother of Martha Boggan. Milford grew up in Simpson County and lived on Boggan Ridge Road. He graduated from Pinola High School and moved to Jackson in 1951. There he was employed by Armstrong Cork and Tile Company for over 22 years. He was a member and deacon of Highland Baptist Church in Jackson.

8. Wilson William Boggan (1916-1999) was the youngest son of the late William Jesse Boggan, Sr. He attended the Boggan

School and "graduated from Pinola High School as the
valedictorian of his class in 1935. He received his BA degree from
John Brown University, Siloam Springs, Arkansas. He later
attended Southwestern Baptist Theological Seminary in Fort
Worth, Texas, and the US Army Chaplain School at Harvard
University."
[Note: Information from the Obituary of Wilson William Boggan]

Wilson was baptized at the age of 10 and called to preach in his
early teens, being licensed in 1936. He was ordained to the
gospel ministry by Macedonia Baptist Church in 1938. He served
as student missionary under the Student Christian Fellowship of
John Brown University and for a time as pastor in several
churches in the Ozarks. "He served as Chaplain in the United
States Army in 1943 and served with the 6th Armored Division.
He received five Battle Stars and a Bronze Star for Meritorious
Service in connection with military operations in France,
Belgium, Luxembourg and Germany."

After leaving the army in 1945, Rev. Boggan became pastor in
Oklahoma and later served "under the Home Mission Board,
SBC, from July 1948 until 1965, working with the Choctaw and
Chickasaw Indians in south central Oklahoma." Failing health
demanded that he leave his work with the Indians and he moved
back to Mississippi where he became pastor of Hurley Baptist
Church in Jackson County, Mississippi. Later he served as
Superintendent of Missions for George County, Greene, and
Wayne Baptist Associations.

Rev. Boggan was married to Jessie Mae Gates. "Although ill a
great deal of the time, Jessie Boggan was a blessing to all with
whom she came in contact. Her death, from five years of illness
with Lymphosarcoma, was a great loss to the work and the life
of Rev. Boggan." Wilson then married Wilma Allbritton Boggan
from Moss Point, Mississippi. "She has a B.S. degree in Music
and a Masters in Elementary Education from University of
Southern Mississippi. The Boggans have four children: Elvis
Wilson, Richard Delton, Elizabeth Luellen" and stepson James
William McLeod.

Although Wilson died in Pascagoula, he and his first wife, Jessie, were buried in the Macedonia Baptist Church Cemetery in Weathersby.
[Source: findagrave.com/memorial/152380798/Wilson-williams-boggan by Richard D. Boggan, contributor 48333236]

After bearing all these children and keeping house for a husband and a total of eleven children, Laura died on May 4, 1929. She was buried in Francis M. Walker Cemetery in Pinola.

The third wife of William Boggan was Ella Smith and there were no further children born in the household. William died on June 25, 1944, and was buried in the Macedonia Baptist Church Cemetery, Weathersby.

The next child born to Alexander B. Boggan and Nancy Jane McLendon was Nancy Jane Boggan, who was born in 1869 and was the first wife of German Washington Gardner. They married on April 14, 1887, and had several children: Leona, Mable Ella, Era Elizabeth [Slay], Walter Clarence, Chesley, Mary Quinnie [Gardner], and Minnie. Nancy died in 1910 and German remarried. His second wife was Susie M. Patrick who helped him raise the younger children.

Leona was born on October 29, 1891, and married Preston Pierce. They had three children:

Ernest Pierce;
Myra Jane Pierce married James Nelson Bailey and had three children:
Carl Glen Bailey;
Sarah Louise Bailey Alford Cothren;
James Carroll Bailey;
Sherwood R. Pierce.

Leona died on April 1, 1966, and was buried in the Bethel Cemetery in Brandon, Mississippi. Preston Pierce died the next year and was buried beside Leona.

Mable Ella Gardner was born on April 14, 1894, and married Alonzo S. Brown. He was employed by the Illinois Central Railroad in Jackson and was transferred to West Monroe, Louisiana, where he changed jobs and worked for Olin Mathieson Chemical Corporation. Ella died in West Monroe in

Kin

August 1987, and after retirement, Alonzo moved back to Jackson where he later died and was buried in Cedar Lawn Cemetery, Jackson.

Era Elizabeth, born on August 13, 1896, married Furman Quinn Slay and they had eight children: Hudson Luther Slay (1918-1996), Eula Jane Slay Mahaffey (1919-2001); Quinn Washington Slay (1922-1989); Ona Belle Slay Dillon (1924-1995); Harold Wayne Slay (1936-1956); Carroll Wallace Slay (1936-2012); Polly Slay Sexton; and Leona Slay. They were members of the Jehovah's Witness Church. Ella died on October 14, 1983, and was buried in the Mendenhall City Cemetery, Mendenhall.

Walter Clarence Gardner was a building contractor in Houston, Texas. He was born on May 10, 1899, in Simpson County and married Velma Elizabeth Puckett. He died on December 24, 1956, in Houston and was buried in the Forest Park Cemetery, Houston.

German Chesley Gardner was born on December 2, 1901, in Simpson County. He was a World War II Veteran and worked for Railway Express Agency in Jackson. He married Jessie Lee Robinson. Chesley died on January 3, 1967, and Jessie died just a couple of weeks later. Both are buried in the City Cemetery in Crystal Springs, Mississippi.

Mary Quinnie was born on November 12, 1903, in Simpson County. She married Chester C. Thornton who was a prominent banker in Jackson. He was Vice President of the Mississippi Bank and Trust Company from its inception until his retirement. He was a member of a number of organizations, including the Capitol Lodge #600, the Shriners and Scottish Rite, and Past Worthy Patron of Eastern Star #47. He was also a deacon of Parkway Baptist Church, where the family were members. Their two daughters were Catherine L. and Carolyn F. Thornton. Quinnie died on April 15, 1983, and was buried in the Cedar Lawn Cemetery in Jackson.

Nancy and German Gardner (or "George" as he was affectionately known) were the parents of Minnie, the last child of seven. Minnie was born about 1906 and trained as a nurse. She married Forest H. Sproles, a fireman. They lived in Jackson and were members of First Baptist Church. Their only child was Forest H. Sproles, Jr. Forest died at age 58 of a heart attack, and Minnie died in 1984.

The next child of Alex and Nancy Boggan was Sarah "Sallie" Ann Boggan who was born on June 1, 1874. She married Robert "Bob" Brown. They had one son whom they named William Gaston Brown. Bob died on May 2, 1897, and several years later Sallie married a man with a house full of children, Draton Malachai Smith, nicknamed "D. C."
[Note: In the information from Nora Byrd D.C.'s middle was Manacar.]

D. C. had three children by his first wife, Mary E. Wigginton:

Lewis Oscar "Slick" Smith;
Tina Lenora Smith;
Arthur Henry Smith.

After Mary's death, D. C. married Sarah "Sallie" Lingle, and they had four more children:

Thomas H. Smith (1900-1983);
Thelma Rachel Smith (1901-1964);
Berta Smith (1903-1989);
Letha Altha Smith (1904-1988).

Sallie died on August 14, 1908, and D.C. quickly married another Sallie, Sarah "Sallie" Ann (or Angeline) Boggan Brown, who had one son. They married in March 1909.

D.C. lived in Mt Olive, Mississippi, so Sallie Brown and her son moved into his home with all his children. Then this Sallie had four more children:

Nora Elizabeth Smith (1910-1993);
Joe Edward Smith (1912-1991) named for Sallie's brother;
Fannie Mae Smith (1914-2006);
Vera Clara Smith (1915-2010).

Sallie and D.C. lived on a farm, and the children worked the land and helped care for the house until each of them married and moved away. D. C. died on November 8, 1935, and is buried in Mt Olive. After his death, Sallie continued to live in her home in Mt. Olive until 1935 when she moved into the home of her daughter, Fannie Mae DeLaughter, in Jackson. She joined the Van Winkle Methodist Church and lived in Jackson until age 79 when she died. Sallie was buried in the Macedonia Baptist Church Cemetery in Simpson County near Mendenhall.

The next child of Alex Boggan and Nancy Boggan was Josiah "Joe" Edward Boggan, who was born on December 19, 1875. He married Lou Dora Weathersby on December 29, 1898, and soon they welcomed their only son, Wallace Edward Boggan, into the world on November 11, 1899. They lived in Simpson County and were members of the Macedonia Baptist Church. Sadly, Lou died on December 12, 1900. Her obituary says that she was "a model Christian lady, kind, loving, possessing that spirit of gentleness; and those who knew her, knew her but to love her."

Later that year Joe married Phenie Egeria Grubbs, born on December 8, 1895. Phenie helped Joe raise Wallace and they had no other children. After her father died, Phenie's mother moved in with them until her death in 1958.

Joe "served 16 years on the Board of Supervisors for Beat 3, Mississippi, and was employed by the Mendenhall Funeral Home for 19 years. He was a member of Westville Masonic Lodge of Pinola" and continued to be a member of Macedonia Baptist Church until his death on January 7, 1961. Phenie lived until October 6, 1976, and both are buried in the Macedonia Baptist Church Cemetery. [Note: Information from Josiah's obituary]

Alex Boggan's last child was Millie Elizabeth "Lizzie" Boggan, born on March 26, 1877. Lizzie married Johnny Garfield Brown and they lived their whole lives in Simpson County. They had five children:

> Curvin Joe Brown was born on July 19, 1925, and died on November 2, 1983, in Merit, Simpson County. Curvin married Myrtle Angie Finch whose younger brother, Noble Curtis Finch, married Curvin's younger sister, Gertrude Elizabeth Brown. Their children were C. J., Jr. and Bobbie, and all their cousins were double first cousins.

> Maude Brown married Henry Columbus Cliburn, a carpenter in Simpson County. They were members of Rials Creek Methodist Church and raised five children:

>> Edward A. Cliburn married Billie Earlene Floyd and they had seven children: Billy Charles Burnham (from

Billie Earlene's first marriage), Sheila, Mary Ann, Angela, Cindy, Cheryl, and Randy.

Vaiden Cliburn married R. T. Barlow and lived in Bogalusa, Louisiana. She was active in several civic organizations and was named Bogalusa's Citizen of the Year in 2008.

Gertrude "Gertie" Cliburn married John Dee McNaughton on March 30, 1982, and they had one son, Johnny D., Jr. This family lived in Jackson, and Gertie was the last sibling to die on June 11, 2018.

Brenda married Jimmy Russell, and Myrtle Lee married William Decovin Means, who was a Home Depot employee.

Emily married Charles Thompson and was the youngest of the six siblings.

Daughter Myrtle Lee Brown was born on November 29, 1905, and married Dewey Curtis May. They had six children: Phenia, Johnie Travis, Grady, Eva Jean, Willie Tillman, and Curvin. Phenia and Tillman lived in Lakeland, Florida, and the rest stayed in Mississippi. Myrtle died in March 1993 in Simpson County and was buried in the Macedonia Baptist Church Cemetery.

Gertrude Elizabeth Brown was a member of Eastern Star, and she and her husband, Noble Curtis Finch, and children David Fonzo and Dorothy Louise Finch were all members of Forest Hills Baptist Church in Hinds County. Gertrude Elizabeth died on September 20, 1990, in Hinds County.

The last child was George Ira Brown and he only lived to be 24 years old. He was born on April 2, 1910, and died on October 13, 1934. He never married. His tombstone reads: "He died as he lived a Christian."

Johnny Garfield died in 1911, but Lizzie lived 57 years longer. She died on January 1, 1968, and was buried, like so many others in this family, in the Macedonia Baptist Church Cemetery.

Kin

In 1876, Alex and Nancy Boggan "purchased, by estate deed, the William 'Buck' McLendon plantation in Mississippi. Their son, William Jesse Boggan and his family made their home with them. Willlam's son, Theo Luther Boggan, continued living in the same house after he married and raised his family there. By 1981 he still owned the place."

Theo remembers his Grandmother Boggan well. He said, "She smoked a corn cob pipe and liked to have it lit by laying a coal of fire on top of the tobacco in the pipe bowl. After she reached a certain age, however, the family did not want her lighting her own pipe because she might catch her clothing on fire or maybe even fall into the fire. It was young Theo's responsibility to keep his grandmother's pipe lit." [Note: Internet story on Ancestry.com]

In addition to the purchase of the family farm, Alex bought another 175.75 acres of Choctaw land in 1896, making him a quite prominent citizen in the Westville area of Simpson County. As the children grew up, married, and bought up land of their own, the Boggans occupied a major portion of the southern part of the county.

Alex died on September 2, 1909, and Nancy died ten years later on August 18, 1919. Both are buried in the Macedonia Baptist Church Cemetery.

Since Margaret Lou Boggan married Lewis B. Ball, and their daughter was Hattie B. Ball, they are the links between the Boggan Family and eventually the Byrd Family. Hattie Ball Brown's daughter Nora married Edward Leavell Byrd completing the connection of these two families.

Sources:
Websites:
    Geni-com/people/Sir-Walter-Boggan/600000000823112134.
    Google Search:
        Alabama, Surname Files Expanded, 102-1981.
        townofwadesboro.org/history-of-wadesboro.html.
    Ancestry.com: The Boggan Family
    AOL.com: members.aol.com/InmanGA/family.mask.
    www.findagrave.com/memorial/152380798/wilson-williams-boggin
    Virginia Boggan Cruse: *The Clark Family*, an Internet Book.
    http://ourworld.cs.com/uptondavid/simpsonfolk/eliving.htm.
    http://home.earthlink.net/~rooo22/simpson1.htm "Reprinted
    from 'Simpson County Sesquicentennial Historical Booklet 1974']
Personal Papers from Nora Brown Byrd.
On-Site Visits

THE BROWN FAMILY

How does the Brown Family relate to the Byrd Family? Edward Leavell Byrd married Nora Beatrice **Brown** on July 16, 1936. This is the story of Nora's paternal Brown family.

For several years the Brown family was a mystery, but an Internet contact shared a great deal of information about the Brown family, some of the information being his and some he gleaned from other researchers. Basically, the family history begins with Samuel Brown, who settled in Augusta, Georgia, in the 1700s and follows the family through their migration into the Alabama/Mississippi Territories.
[Source: Dickie Grubbs at Dickiegrubbs@hotmail.com]

Samuel Brown, Sr. was an "Indian Trader." Although the exact responsibilities and activities of an Indian trader are not known, it is presumed that he basically traded goods with the Indians. His place of birth is also unknown, although speculation would have him emigrating to the United States from England. He was born prior to 1696. He was also married, but his wife's name is unknown, and she is thought to have died in England prior to Samuel's emigration. One notation furnished by Dickie Grubbs says, "On June 14, 1736, (Samuel Brown) had orders from Mr. James Oglethorpe for a 500-acre lot and house in Fort Augusta, GA." Apparently, Samuel lived in Augusta, St. Paul's Parish, Georgia, in the 1730s.

Another notation about Samuel appears in some papers from Lt. Kent, Commander of Fort Augusta, written in September 1738:

> *March 1738: Mr. Samuel Brown, one of our Indian Traders, being newly come to town out of the Cherokee Nation, principally to take some advice about a wound which he got in his head among his fellow traders, was at the club this evening when I went thither, and he gave me the following relation viz.- That besides the 500 acres of land he had at Augusta, and which he was intent upon improving of, there was a small island lying in the river [Savannah River], betwixt that and New Windsor (and therefore in the Province of Georgia) which he said Mr. Oglethorpe had granted him to hold by lease, and that he had put several people upon it to cultivate land; but that the Carolina Governor of New Windsor had taken an opportunity to drive all his men off, alleging*

that it was part of Carolina, and he would plant it himself. I could say little to it, but thought it worth notice here.

In the book, *Early Settlers in Georgia* (by George Gillman Smith, D.D.) in 1901, there is information about the Indian traders near Augusta, Georgia.

Before Mr. Oglethorpe came to Georgia, there was a trading post near what is now Hamburg, S.C., on the South Carolina side of the river, called Fort Moore and Mr. Oglethorpe dedicated to build a fort on the Georgia side and garrison it. This he did, and in honor of the Princess Augusta, it was called by her name.

*In the pamphlet...by Wm. Stephens, there is the following list of Indian traders who had headquarters at Augusta. The names given are: Wood, **Brown** [emphasis by author], Clark, Knott, Spencer, Barnett, Ladson, Mackey, Elsey, Facy, McQueen, Wright, Gardner, Andrews, Duvall, Cammell, Randel, Chauncey, Newberry.*

On the east side of the Savannah, in South Carolina, there were numbers of plantations opened, and the corn consumed by the large number of horses needed in the trade with the Indians was produced there.

These Indian traders sent out their men to the towns of the Chickasaws, Uchees, Creeks, and Cherokees, and in the spring season, great crowds of Indians came with their ponies loaded with peltry to trade at the post for powder and lead, and especially for rum.

There was a mean rum, known as tafia, which was the main article of traffic. It was brought by Indian traders from the coast and traded for all kinds of products and for Indian slaves. These slaves, taken by their enemies in war, were brought to Augusta and sold and carried to Charleston and shipped to the West Indies.

The traders were oftentimes wretchedly dissolute. They lived shameless lives with the squaws, and when they grew weary of them, went from them without hesitation...

Kay Byrd

The date of death and the place of burial for Samuel Brown is not known, but it is assumed that his grave is somewhere near the location of Fort Augusta, Georgia.

Samuel Brown, Sr., was the father of **Samuel Brown, Jr.,** who was born in Bristol, England, about 1715. Like his father, Samuel, Jr. was an Indian trader, but he lived in Savannah, Georgia, on "Lot 51." Samuel married a young lady named Mary [last name unknown], and they had either four or five children. The children of Samuel and Mary Brown were:

William Brown (born in 1729 or 1730) who fought in the Revolutionary War and settled in Washington County, GA;

Thadiers (or Thaddeus) Brown;

A Daughter whose name is unknown;

Samuel Brown (III?) born sometime between 1737 and 1742 probably in Savannah and who migrated to Mississippi;

John Brown [There is some doubt about John Brown. He might have been Samuel's son, although he was probably his brother.]

Samuel Brown (III?) was a person of interest. He married a widow, Mary Mooney Hickson, whose first husband [William Hickson] had died in the Revolutionary War. Mary had children with her first husband: A daughter named Keziah Hickson and a son named William Hickson. Mary was born in Pennsylvania on April 18, 1747, the daughter of Joseph and Mary Moore Mooney, Sr. Her parents moved to Wrightsboro [or Wrightsborough], Columbia County, Georgia, sometime between 1740 and 1774.

Samuel Brown served in the Revolutionary War and was awarded a certificate from Colonel G. Lee on the 26th of April, 1784, entitling him to a "bounty of 250 acres of land and pay for same in Washington County, Georgia." [Customarily, soldiers of the Revolutionary War received land grants as pay for their services. Information about Samuel Brown was found in the DAR Patriot Index, Page 93. He is listed as "Sol GA," interpreted as Soldier from Georgia.]

In addition, there is recorded in the land deeds for Richmond County, Georgia, the following information:

Samuel Brown – Two hundred acres of land in Richmond Co., GA. North by Vacant Land, east by said Browns Land, and Lands Vacant Southwardly by or near Peter Perkins Land, and West by James Moore and Vacant Land. July 25, 1787. [By this we know that Samuel already had land joining this additional 200 acres.]

Samuel and Mary were the parents of eight children:

Isham Brown, born May 14, 1784;
Cecilia Brown, married John Brown;
Hezekiah Brown, married Mary Handley;
Kireah (or Keziah) Brown, married John Thomas in Smith
    County, Mississippi;
Emilia Brown, married Unknown Copeland;
Solomon Brown;
Elizabeth Brown, married Joseph Chapman in Rankin,
    County, Mississippi;
John Brown married "Unknown".

Samuel Brown and some of his male relatives decided to move their families to the new Alabama/Mississippi Territory. The land was attractive and the price was cheap. "After 1815 the American economy began to expand rapidly. The cotton boom in the South spread settlement swiftly across the Gulf Plains: The Deep South was born. Practically all Indians east of the Mississippi were placed on small reservations or forced to move to the Great Plains beyond the Missouri River. Canals and railroads opened the interior to swift expansion, both of settlement and trade. In the Midwest many new cities, such as Chicago, appeared and enormous empires of wheat and livestock farms came into being. From 1815 to 1850 a new western state entered the Union, on average, every 2 ½ years. By 1820 all the lands east of the Mississippi River had been carved into separate states or territories. The territory of Mississippi, with its capital at Natchez, was organized in 1798 and in 1817. Mississippi became the 20th state.
[Source:www.users.qwest.net/~willmurray/Murray/simpson_county_miss issippi_...]

"The development of early emigrant trails more or less followed well-established trails made by wild animals in search of food or water. These trails were well worn upon the earth before man came along. In search of basic necessities, the American Indian followed these same trails, and eventually they were used by the Indians for barter/commerce, social visits, and sometimes for purposes of war or adventure. Eventually, when the white man came, either on foot or horseback, and when the Indians would permit, he used the same trails. Many portions were later followed successfully by wagon trains and even to the present, some are now turnpikes and highways." [Source: See Above]

The following information was found in Georgia court records for Wednesday, November 13, 1811:

Ordered that passports be prepared for the following persons to travel through The Indian Nations to the Western County viz...Thaddeus Brown, Isham Brown, Samuel Brown with two negroes and John Brown with six negroes, all from the county of Washington in this State of Georgia.

The Brown family "most likely followed...The Lower Creek Trading Path...from Augusta...to Macon, Georgia. There they would have picked up *The Macon & Montgomery Trail* to Montgomery, Alabama, and from there they most likely turned more southwest on *The Alabama and Mobile Trail* since they settled first in Wayne County, which is on the border of Alabama and Mississippi." [www.users.qwest.net...]

Sometime between 1820-1830, Samuel and Isham, his son, and their families moved to the future Simpson County, approximately seventy miles to the west of Wayne County, settling on Rials Creek. "Simpson County lies in the southern half of Mississippi about midway between the Mississippi River and the Alabama state line. Mendenhall, the current county seat, is thirty-one miles southeast of Jackson and 125 miles north of the Gulf of Mexico. At the time of its organization, Simpson County was one of the most attractive counties of the great Southwest and that is why, for the first 21 years after its establishment, it grew so rapidly in population. Doubtless the early settlers from Scotland, New England, Virginia and the Carolinas sent back to their relatives glowing accounts of this new country."
[Source: www.users.qwest.net...)

"The attractions of this area were many and varied. First of all, of course, was the fact that homesteads could be had for the asking, and the lands on the creeks and rivers were very fertile. Another attraction was the abundance of running water: beautiful, clear running streams, wonderful springs bubbling up on the hills. Especially notable were the great springs at Rials that formed a creek at the very beginning."
[Source: www.rootsweb.com/~mssimpson/)

"The greatest of attractions, however, were the great pine forests that covered the county from the north to the south and from east to west. For miles and miles, one could ride through the untold thousands of trees, standing in their solemnity, magnificent in their grandeur as they had stood for ages. It seems a sacrilege for them to be destroyed. We shall never see their like again."
[Source: www. rootsweb. com/ ~mmsimpson/)

"Simpson County, with Mendenhall eventually as the county seat, was organized in 1824, seven years after statehood. The population at the time was 2,329 whites and 829 slaves...The county was named for Josiah Simpson, a former Pennsylvanian, educated at Princeton. He later lived at Green Hill, near Natchez, and became a territorial judge of Mississippi and served as a member of the Constitutional Convention of 1917."
[Source: www.rootsweb.com/~mmsimpson/)

Dickie Grubbs says,

> The first settlement made on Rials Creek was made by Gideon Rials (or Rayals). The next was made by Samuel Brown, who settled near the headwaters of this creek. In 1835 Samuel Brown was elected to serve as Representative from Simpson County in the Mississippi State Legislature. He was a prominent resident of the county, but he and Mary Ann were the only white persons living on Rials Creek in 1837. They owned several negroes and were generally thought to have a considerable amount of money.

> On the night of September 10, 1837, three Negroes, all of whom bore the name Henry and a woman by the name of Rose murdered Samuel and Mary (who were very old – about 90-100 years old at the time) for their money. Two or three of their Negro slaves were also killed to prevent their testifying against the murderers. A white man by the name of Miller was charged with having instigated the murder and was alleged to have received

the greater part of the money. He was prosecuted for the crime. Three of the Negroes (two of the Henrys) and the colored woman Rose, were convicted of the murder and hanged by William J. Toler, who was then Sheriff, near the place where T. J. Peacock lived. A change of venue was obtained in Miller's case to Hinds County where he died in jail before there was any final disposition of the case.

The exact location of the burial place of Samuel and Mary Brown is not known. On August 29, 1937, J. P. Edwards (Great-great grandson of Samuel) delivered a *History of the Brown Family* at a Brown reunion. The family decided to place a monument on the graves of Samuel and Mary, but it is unknown whether or not this is the actual site of their graves. It is located near the head of Rials Creek on property once owned by Samuel. It is near the foot of a knoll where the homestead once stood.

To find the monument a guide is needed. (Contact: Gerald Brown at 436 Rials Creek Road, Mendenhall, Mississippi 39114; 601-849-3403, Magee Listing). The marker is a small granite stone (approx. 30'x21'x6' out of the ground). Directions: Start at the junction of Airport Road and Rials Creek Road. Go east on Airport one mile and on the right side of the road (south) is an aluminum gate. About ¼ mile south of the gate at the bottom of a knoll the marker can be found.
[Source: Dickiegrubbs@hotmail.com and "Historical Tribute Paid to Samuel and Mary Brown" by Dan H. Johnson at alssar.org/Brown GraveMarking.htm]

The Will of Samuel Brown was found in the Mississippi Court Records from the files of the *High Court of Errors and Appeals*, 1799-1859 (Ref: Genealogy 976.2 He; Pages 260-261) by Laura Flanagan (laLynn@aol.com). It is as follows:

Will of Samuel Brown

I, Samuel Brown, of the County of Simpson, State of Mississippi, being in good health of body and of sound and disposing mind and memory (praise be God for the same) and being desirous to settle my worldly affairs whilst I have strength and capacity so to do, make and publish this my last Will and Testament, hereby revoking and making void all former wills, deeds of gift by me at any time heretofore made; and first and principally I commit my soul into the hands of the Creator, who gave it and my body to the earth to be entered in the burying ground of my land at the same place in which James J. Irby's child is buried at the discretion of my executor herein-after named. And as to such worldly goods it hath pleased God to intrust [sic] me with, I dispose of the same as follows:

I give and bequeath to my beloved daughter, Cecilia Brown, five dollars of my estate,

   To my beloved son John Brown five dollars of my estate,

   To my son Hezekiah Brown five dollars of my estate,

   To my daughter Kireah Thomas five dollars of my estate,

   To my daughter Emilia Copeland five dollars of my estate, and

   To Solomon Brown five dollars of my estate, and

   To my daughter Elizabeth Chapman five dollars of my estate,

   To my beloved son, Isham Brown, all of my estate of every kind whatsoever real or personal after giving the other heirs their legal dowry; to wit all my lands, negroes, all my horses, all my cattle, all my hogs, sheep, household furniture, farming utensils, which I may die possessed of (except one little negro girl Evaline, which negro girl I hereby give and bequeath to my nephew, Samuel Carson Brown).

But all of my estate aforesaid is to remain in my possession as fully and entirely as though this my will had not been published during my natural life, and in case my wife, Mary Brown, should survive me, the same is hereby granted to her during her natural life.

And I hereby appoint my beloved son, Isham Brown, my sole executor of this my last will and testament, hereby expressly revoking all former wills by me made.

In witness hereof I have hereunto set my hand and seal the twenty-second day of February in the year of our Lord One Thousand Eight Hundred and Thirty-seven.

                    His Mark: Samuel X Brown

Signed, Sealed and Published and Delivered
by the above-named Samuel Brown to be
his last will and testament
in the presence of us
who have hereunto subscribed
our name as witnesses in the presence of the testator:

James J. Irby
John Brown (This may have been witnessed by John Brown's son,
Littleberry Brown rather than by John Brown himself.)

Proved in Probate Court of Simpson County, Mississippi: December Term
1837

A quick reading of this Will would help anyone understand why the Will was contested upon the death of Samuel Brown. In addition to their parents having died a cruel and tragic death, the heirs were disappointed at receiving a mere five dollars each [even though five dollars in those days might have been more valuable than in today's world]. Certainly, Isham Brown was pleased and was eventually awarded the majority of his parents' estate, as described in the Will, by the Mississippi Supreme Court.

Isham Brown, Sr., was born on May 14, 1784, in Richmond County, Georgia. He was a Methodist minister and a farmer/ planter. He married Mary Ann Grimes [born February 15, 1794, in Georgia], the daughter of Samuel Dawson Grimes of North Carolina and Darcus Wall of Wake County, North Carolina. [Note: S. D. and Darcus Grimes were members of the Primitive Baptist Church outside Troy, Pike County, Alabama, where they settled after leaving Georgia.]

Isham and Mary Ann were married in Georgia and were the proud parents of fourteen children, the first of whom were presumably twins:

Dorcas and Elizabeth Brown, born in 1810; Dorcas married
John Tullos; Elizabeth married Basil Puckett;
Mary Ann "Polly" Brown, 1812, married Thomas Evan Hutson;
lived near Mayton, Mississippi, and died in 1881;
Sarah Brown, 1813, married Pete Stubbs;
Felix Grimes Brown, 1813 (maybe 1814?), married Adeline
Tullos;
John (Johnny) Purdom Brown, born November 18, 1816; first
married Martha Williamson and then Simmie Pernice;
Alfred Brown, 1818;
Solomon Brown, 1820; married Katherine Williamson, was
buried in the Macedonia Cemetery – Rials Creek – rural
Mendenhall, Mississippi;
Samuel Dawson Brown, 1824, married Frances J. Hamrick;
lived in Plumb Creek, Caldwell County, Texas;
William Clark Brown, February 21, 1826, married Maneria

Williamson;
Willis Thomas Brown, 1831, married Martha Jane Easterling, and lived in Johnson City, Texas; died in 1872 in Johnson City, Blanco Co., Texas
Hezekiah Brown, 1834;
Allen Grimes Brown, 1836; married Sarah Sallie Gardner;
Elias Brown, 1838.

As a farmer/planter and, after his parents' death, a rather rich landowner, **Isham Brown** now owned a number of slaves. One of these slaves was Manda Boggan and years after Isham's death, she gave an interview which has been preserved and located via the Internet [www.angelfire.com/wi2 familytree/ Brn00002. Html]:

Manda Boggan, ex-slave, lives two miles east of Weathersby, Mississippi. She was born about 1847, was owned during slavery time by Isham Brown in Simpson County. She is small and withered. Her health is very good considering her age. She is a devout Christian but a bit flighty in mind. She sings religious songs one minute while the next will dance as she sings some Negro ragtime song.

I believes I had de bes' master in de worl'. I gits ter thinking' ob de days back in slavery time an' wishes ole Mars could ev alwa's care fo' us. He was a preacher an' sho' did live his religion, an' taught us slaves in de straight an' narrow way. He wouldn't low no overseer wukin' his slaves, 'cause he wont gwine ter hab' 'em beat. He got wuk a plinty out'en us, fer when yo' turn a bunch ob niggers a-lose an' let 'em sing, an' shout all dey wants ter he's gwine ter turn de wuk off.

I don't know who Mars bought my mudder from, but I knows my pa was bought from a man in Virginia. He married my mudder after he come to Mars' plantation. Dey lived in one of de little log cabins back of Mars' who lived in a big low, ramblin' log house wid a big kitchen an' dinin' room built away from de main house. Dey had a slave cook what was named Hannah, dat done the cookin' fer Mars' family an' all de wukin slaves. I jes' wish I could tell you' all ob all de good grub deir was cooked an' served. All I can say is dat hit was good grub in 'bundance.

Kay Byrd

Afore I was big 'nuf to be sent to the filds, I jes' played 'round ever wher wid de chillums. Us made play houses under de big oak trees. Us raked up big piles ob leaves fer beds, an' made rag-dolls. Us made dresses an' hats out'en leaves pined tergether wid pine straws. Den us played run and ketch games us made up.

My first wuk was 'round Mars' house, totin' cule water a mile from a spring, an' milkin' de cows. Hit took a heap ob us ter milk all dem cows. De milk den had to be strained in big stone crocks and put in de daries dat was bilt out under de trees ter keep de milk cool. Deir was a heap o'churnin' ter be done. Hit 'peared lak us had ter churn fer hours 'afore dat butter would be deir.

When I was put in de fields, hit was wuk from early till late. De fields would be full o'slaves a-wuker' hard. Us would look up and see Mars a-comin' across de field wid his Bible under his arm. He would walk along wher us was a-wukin' an' read a text, den us would sing an' pray. De song us laked bes' was "De Day of Jubilee es coms." (Here she sings the song.)

Eber Sunday mornin' Mars went to de slave cabins an' read a de Bible an' prayed. He come in de cabins wid a smile. Us went to meetin' once a month wid de white folks an' set in the back. Us waited on 'em, toted in water an' tended ter de chillums. When de meetin' was ober, us kotched de horses an' led 'em to deir blocks an' brung de carriages 'round fer 'em.

I wants yo' all ter know, us had had gran' times at the frolics. On Sunday nites us would dance all nite long. I can hear dem fiddles an' guitars yet wid dat loud, "swing yo' pardners." Hit was all gran'.'

One ob de saddest days of us' lives was when Ole Mars died. He was de bes' friend us all had or eber will hab. After he was buried in de ole church yard, de slave was divided amoungst his chillum. My dear brother was took slap off to Texas an' us ain't neber heard ob him since. A heap ob de families was tore apart lak dat.

Kin

De war come an' up-sat eber thing, wus den eber. Wid de Yankees a-comin' through a tearing up be whole face ob de earth an' a-takin' eber thing a-gwine an' a-comin'. Den wid de soldiers a-marchin' 'round a-scarin' us slap ter death, us run fas' as us could eber time us seed 'em. When de war git so clos' us could hear de guns a-shootin' and us could see the lights from de battles, I can tell yo' all den was scary dats.

After the war was ended, Ole Missus, she deeded us a little tract ob land an' one of de slave cottages. Us don very well. But I uped an' married the sorriest nigger in the whole country. We raised a big bunch of chillums, an' he died an' I was crazy 'nough ter marry another nigger, who turnt out ter be as sorry as de fust one.

Ise a-livin' wid my daughter now. Ise ole but enjies life. I wuks a little 'round de house. I sings, prays and dances when I gits happy.

De government helps ter take care o' me an' de good white folks helps me long too, a heap o' folk gib me nickels an' dimes ter see me dance.

I believe in ghos'. Seein' is believin' and Ise seed haints all my life. I knows folks can be hoo-dooded, might curious things can be done. One nite I was gwine to a dance. We had ter go through thick woods. Hit was one o' dem nites dat yo' feels lak deir is somethin' somewhars, yo' feels lack an' jumpy an' wants ter look ober yo' shoulder but scart to. Deys alwa a haint 'round when hits lak dat. De fust thing us knowned deir was a ghos' right in front ob us that looked lak a cow. Hit jess stood deir a-gittin bigger an' bigger, den it disappeared. Us run lak something wild. I went on ter dat dance but sho didn't dance none. I just set 'round an' look on, an' from dat nite I ain't neber gone to a frolic an' danced to mo.' Nor I ain eber gwine to.

Isham Brown and his wife had a large family, and most of his children had large families. Several children moved to Texas with their families; but many of the others, as well as many of the grandchildren, stayed in the Simpson County area. There are a number of Browns buried in the Macedonia Baptist Church Cemetery, which is near Rials Creek in rural Mendenhall, Mississippi. Many are buried in the Rials Creek Methodist

Church Cemetery as well as in the "Jim" Reed Cemetery, and others are buried in nearby cemeteries in the same general area.

Since Isham Brown was a Methodist preacher, it is almost certain that his children worshipped in Methodist churches. However, since a goodly number of the family was buried in the Macedonia Baptist Church Cemetery, it is assumed that some of the children became Baptists.

Isham Brown died on December 29, 1862 [during the Civil War] at his home in Simpson County. Mary Ann, his wife, died on July 28, 1865. They are buried in the Rials Creek Methodist Church Cemetery, but no markers are standing on their graves.

Allen Grimes Brown was born in 1830 and died in 1891. Since his parents moved to Mississippi in 1811 and were located in Simpson County in the 1820s, it is almost certain that Allen was born in Simpson County. Like his father and siblings, Allen worked as a farmer and lived his entire life in the Mendenhall area. According to the 1870 U. S. Census, Allen Brown owned 200 acres, was married to Sarah Sallie Gardner and was the father of five sons and three daughters.

> Samuel "Sam" Brown, born in 1842, moved to Texas;
> Mary Louisa Brown, born November 2, 1866,
> died January 22, 1940, married William Elijah Colman;
> James Alvie Brown, 1868-1893, married Loura B. May;
> Robert "Bob" L. Brown, November 2, 1874, died May 20, 1897, married
> Sarah Angeline "Sallie Ann" Boggan;
> Burtie Brown born December 26, 1872, engaged to Ike May, died in a
> fire at age 20;
> Sarah Lottie Brown, born September 22, 1878, died July 30, 1925;
> married Thomas Busick;
> Johnny Garfield Brown, born February 8, 1881, died January 26, 1911,
> married Elizabeth "Lizzie" Boggan, five children:
>> Curvin Joe Brown, born November 11, 1901;
>> Maude Brown, born May 14, 1904;
>> Myrtle Lee Brown, born November 29, 1905;
>> Gertrude Elizabeth Brown, born June 6, 1908, in Mendenhall, MS,
>> married Noble Curtis Finch (1906-1965) and died in Jackson, MS;
>> George Ira Brown, born April 22, 1910.

George Matthew Brown, born January 22, 1887, died February 9, 1917, married Hattie Jane Ball.

George Matthew Brown

George Matthew Brown's wife, Hattie Jane Ball, was the granddaughter of Alexander and Nancy Jane McClendon, and the daughter of Margaret Lou Boggan and Louis B. Ball. George and Hattie had four children:

> Sarah Lessie Brown, born November 2, 1908; died September 19, 1922;
> Mary Letha Brown, born August 22, 1910; died March 2, 1948;
> Nora Beatrice Brown, born July 6, 1912; died June 25, 1998;
> John Grady Brown, born February 28, 1914; died December 18, 1978.

[Source: www.angelfire.com/wi2/familytree/Brn00004.html]

[NOTE: For several years the relationship between Nora Brown Byrd and Pat Herrington Dickmann was a mystery. Research into the Brown Family has revealed the answer, but it is complicated.

George Matthew Brown had a first cousin named Solomon Brown who was 37 years George's senior. Solomon had a daughter named Mattie Brown who married Joseph Patterson. Their daughter was Beulah "Pat" Patterson. Pat Patterson married Samuel O. Herrington; and when he died, she married Bernard "Bernie" F. Dickmann, who became the Mayor of St. Louis.

George's daughter Nora and Solomon's granddaughter Pat were kin. They were not first or second cousins and were not even first or second cousins "once removed," but suffice it to say, they were cousins of some sort!]

George was a 32nd degree Mason. As a young man he developed tuberculosis and died at the early age of thirty, on February 9, 1917. He is buried at the Macedonia Baptist Church Cemetery near Mendenhall, Mississippi. [Directions to the cemetery: From Tom Berry Road, turn left onto Frank McLendon. Turn Left on Athens and then Right on Macedonia. The Macedonia Baptist Church is on Macedonia Road.]

Since Hattie had not worked outside the home, she had no means of income after her husband died. As the widow of a Mason, however, she and her children were eligible for the Masonic Widows and Orphans Home

Kay Byrd

in Meridian, Mississippi. Apparently, widows were expected to help pay for their family's room and board, so Hattie went to work in the Home's laundry. With this job she could stay near her children during the day and be with them at night. However, when her elder daughter, Lessie, contracted tuberculosis and was no longer welcome in the Home, Hattie had to leave her work and take Lessie to live elsewhere. Presumably, they moved in with relatives. Later, after Lessie died and as the other children aged and left the Home, Hattie lived with various relatives until her son was old enough to support her.

Sarah Lessie Brown was buried in a pauper's grave (Masonic Lot, Grave #5) in the Magnolia Cemetery which is adjacent to the old Masonic Home property in Meridian, Mississippi.

In the orphanage, the children remained close to each other. Nora said, she and Grady used to caution each other to "hold up your shoulders" and "don't slouch." At some point, Grady was sent to live on a farm, and it was on the farm that he was severely treated. He worked hard all day and was the recipient of harsh punishments and little or no loving care. In the meantime, the sisters, became very close during this period.

When time came for college, both Letha and Nora were permitted to attend Mississippi State College for Women in Columbia, Mississippi. They began college during the Great Depression, and as money became less and less available, the Home realized they could not afford to send both girls back to college. Since Nora had better grades, she was the one chosen to complete college. However, she was forced to transfer to Mississippi College for Women, a Baptist institution in Hattiesburg, Mississippi, where the costs were cheaper.

Mary Letha, a pretty, brown-haired young woman, married Felix Daughtery Wilder (born on December 18, 1901), who was about nine years older than she. They had no children, and they lived in a house several miles out of Meridian, Mississippi, in the town of Toomsuba. Their house was built up on pillars in the rear. They parked their car under the porch overhang and walked up a long staircase to their living quarters above. Felix raised turkeys and, although Letha was unaware of the danger, she was probably allergic to the turkey feathers, the mites, and/or the dust surrounding the turkeys. Like her father and older sister, Letha developed tuberculosis, spent time in the sanatorium near Mt. Olive, and died in her late 30s on March 2, 1948. She was also buried in the Magnolia Cemetery in Meridian near her sister Lessie's grave.

Felix remarried after Letha's death. His new wife was Geneva Pearl Bounds, whose first husband was Charles Fletcher Hughes. Felix died on November 12, 1981, and is buried in Magnolia Cemetery. He had lived to be 79 years old. Geneva outlived Felix by sixteen years, dying at age 95 on February 4, 2006. She is also buried in Magnolia Cemetery.

Nora Beatrice Brown was born on July 6, 1912, in Weathersby, and like her sister and brother, she grew up in the Widows and Orphans Home in Meridian. She graduated from the Mississippi College for Women in Hattiesburg in 1935 with a degree in French and was described in the school yearbook as "poised, attractive, self-assured; she does everything well."

Her first job was a teaching position in Mount Olive, Mississippi, where she met her future husband, Edward Leavell Byrd. They married on July 16, 1936, at the First Baptist Church in Mt. Olive.

Nora and Edward were the parents of three children:

> Edward Leavell Byrd, Jr., born on September 19, 1937, and died on November 23, 1994;
> Hersey Davis Byrd, born on February 22, 1942;
> Beatrice Joy Byrd Rich, born on September 28, 1949.

Edward was an ordained Baptist minister, and with her outgoing personality and love of people, Nora was the perfect pastor's wife. They served in three full-time churches until retirement: In Holly Springs and Meridian, Mississippi; and in Florence, South Carolina.

Nora died of cancer on June 25, 1998, and Edward died six years later on January 22, 2004. Both are buried in Mt. Hope Cemetery in Florence, South Carolina. [Note: For more information on Nora, see the book, *Oaks of Righteousness,* by Kay M. Byrd]

After a sad, harsh childhood at the Widows and Orphans Home in Meridian, John Grady Brown graduated from high school around 1932, and he and his mother shared a rental home in Jackson. During World War II, Grady was drafted, enlisting in the U.S. Army on April 11, 1942. He served until December 5, 1945.

On November 25, 1943, Grady married Dorothy "Dot" Lucille Diffenderfer. Dot was the daughter of Raleigh and Lola Mae Benham Diffenderfer. Her father was born in Illinois and her mother in Indiana, but they moved to Mississippi and bought a farm in Yazoo County. They had nine children, and for some years, the children's Diffenderfer grandmother lived with them as well.

After the war Grady owned and operated a sheet metal business, and Dot worked at the Mississippi Baptist Hospital. They always had a vegetable garden, and Dot cooked wonderful "Southern comfort" food.

Two children were born to Grady and Dot: Joyce Marie Brown was born on December 22, 1946, and she married Paul Leland Bradshaw on July 24, 1971. **George Raleigh Brown** was born August 27, 1950; and he married Louise Gordon. Grady and Dot's family was a happy one, and they always graciously welcomed visits from family members.

Grady liked country music, but his sister Nora was not much of a fan. When Grady played a country song, he would jokingly say to Nora, "Now, Nora, you know that's 'purty' music."

Like his father, Grady was a Mason and a member of the Plains [Mississippi] A&FM Lodge #622. He was also a member of the Order of the Eastern Star in Plainview, Mississippi; and both Dot and Grady were members of the First Baptist Church of Richland.

Grady died of cancer on December 18, 1978, and was buried in the Lakewood South Memorial Park in Jackson. Some years after Grady's death, Dot married William Henry Turcotte (born January 24, 1917, in Magee). Bill was an interesting man and a bird-watching enthusiast. Dot and Bill enjoyed many bird-watching trips as long as their health allowed.

Bill Turcotte had been a prisoner of war during World War II and imprisoned in a German *Stalag*. The experiences were so devastating that he could barely talk about them. During his captivity he was able to draw pictures of his experiences, and he was able to share these pictures in later life with others.

Bill was a Wildlife Biologist Administrator and a member of the 8th Air Force Memorial Society, the DAV 91st Bomb Group Memorial Association, the American Ex-Prisoner of War Association, Stalag Three Former POW Association, and a charter member of the Mississippi Museum of Natural

Science Foundation. He died of cancer on November 5, 2000, and is buried in the Clinton Cemetery in Clinton, Hinds County, Mississippi, near his first wife.

In July 1950, Hattie Ball Brown (Whitlock) died and was buried beside her first husband, George Matthew Brown, in the Macedonia Baptist Church Cemetery near Weathersby and Mendenhall, Mississippi.

George and Louise Brown had three children, two daughters and one son. Their son, Leigh, is the last Brown in this family and therefore the family name lives on. Nora Brown Byrd is the link, however, between the Brown family and the Byrd family.

Sources:
Websites:
>   Dickie Grubbs: Dickiegrubbs@hotmail.com
>   Dan H. Johnson: "Historical Tribute Paid to Samuel and Mary Brown" at alssar.org/BrownGraveMarking.htm.
>   Genealogytrails.com/geo/state/1740earlysettlers.htm
>   Google Search: Papers from Lt. Kent, Commander of Fort Augusta
>   Internet Search: Land Deeds: Richmond County, Georgia
>   www.angelfire.com/wi2/familytree/Brn00004.html
>   www.users.gwest.net~willmurray/Murray/simpson_conty_missi ssippi...
>   www.rootsweb.com/~missimpson/
>   Mississippi Court Records, *High Court of Errors and Appeals*, 1799-1859, (Ref: Genealogy 976.2He; Pages 260-261)
>   laLynn@aol.com
>   www.angelfire.com/wi2/familytree/Brn00002.html
>   Ancestry.com
>   MyHeritage.com
>   FamilySearch.com,
Personal Visits, Interviews and Observations

Kay Byrd

THE DUCKWORTH FAMILY

How does the Duckworth family relate to the Byrd family? Kisiah Duckworth married Josiah Rogers, and their daughter was Mary Malissa Rogers who married John King Byrd. The eldest Byrd son was James Edward, and he married Effie Leona McNeil. Their son was Edward Leavell Byrd, the father of Hersey Davis Byrd.

John Duckworth

John Duckworth was born in Whalley, Lancastershire, England in 1645. He emigrated to the American Colonies as a four-year indentured servant in 1664. In his book, *Rogers-Rodgers: Westward from the Carolinas*, William Morrow Brown quoted the emigration notation found in early colonial records:

> The names of such p'sons as were imported into this province and brought to bee Registered in the Secretary's books of Records are as follows: ...Upon the Account of Wm. Dockwra: ...John Duckworth...
> [Source: 1 Dec 1684: New Jersey: *Patents and Deeds and Other Early Records of New Jersey 1664-1703* by William Nelson, page 61]

John settled in New Jersey. He married Ann Hopewell, born in 1665 in Calver, Maryland, and died in 1731 in St. Mary's County, Maryland. They had at least one son whom they named William Duckworth.

William Duckworth

William Duckworth was born about 1665 in Burlington, New Jersey, and was a yeoman/farmer.

> [Note: The term yeoman refers to farmers and county gentlemen who volunteered to serve in the British Territorial Army. The yeomen soldiers wore old-time uniforms and carried swords and halberds (a combination spear and battleax).
> [Source: "Duckworth History" posted by TamiGaugler51 at ancestry.com]

William married Grace Cook Hunt, and they had six children: John, William, George, Mary, Joseph, and Anna. [More information on these children follows]

William served in the New Jersey militia in 1715 and was in the 5th Company of Colonel Thomas Fermer's New Jersey Regiment during the Revolutionary War.

William died in March 1717 in New Hanover, Burlington County, New Jersey. His estate was appraised by Asher Cleayton, John Wright, and Jonathan Fowler on March 15, 1727. William Cook gave bond on March 15, 1727, as the administrator of the William Duckworth estate. Interestingly, the accounting of William's estate included charges for "sundrys furnished to the widow in her last sickness, two coffins and digging two graves."
[Source: Will Book 1713-1734, page 162: Virginia Genealogist, vol. 4, page 70 as posted on ancestry.com]

Before Grace Duckworth died, she appointed William Bowgar and William Dean as guardians of her young children, Joseph, Anna and Mary Duckworth. The County Court of New Burlington, New Jersey, confirmed this appointment in their May 1728 term. The older children were grown and on their own at this time.

Children of William and Grace were:

1. **John:** Married Sarah Hankins and was a farmer in Frederick County, Virginia. He was appointed constable in Frederick County in 1753, and he requested 400 acres of "waste/ungranted land" from the Proprietor's Office in 1753, which was granted but no action taken until after the Revolutionary War. In 1789 he was granted 400 acres plus an additional eighty.

He was named "overseer of the road" from a Captain Jacob Funk's property to his property in 1755, and he died intestate on April 5, 1757. His widow applied as administrator of his estate which was approved.

After John died in 1757, Sarah and the children moved to Mecklenburg County, North Carolina, around 1768. She married John Hern in Lincoln County on October 9, 1769, and died there in 1804. She is buried in Olney Presbyterian Cemetery in Gastonia.

John and Sarah had three sons: John, William, and Simon; and two daughters, Sally and Rebecca.

2. William: Unlike his brother John, there are numerous notations for William Duckworth. He was quite a scoundrel. First, he married two different women in 1731. His first marriage to Hannah Clevenger apparently ended abruptly since he married again four months later. It is not known what happened to Hannah. She might have died, or her husband could have been a different William Duckworth. At any rate, William married Mary Wright in December of that year, although he later claimed they were never married. From his deathbed, he told a witness to his will that he had bought a marriage license, and he and Mary Wright went to the minister's (or Justice of the Peace) home to be married, but no one was at home. So, they just went home and told everyone they were married. When this deathbed will was produced, however, there were witnesses who swore they had been present at the marriage.

William and Mary had a number of children, the eldest son being Urial Duckworth. William left his wife and family and moved to Fredrick County, Virginia, where he purchased 235 acres of land, but because of poor record-keeping in those days, he might have purchased the same 235 acres twice.

William had served as the co-signer of a bond for Elizabeth Baxter when she applied as Administrator of her brother James Danford's estate. Apparently, it was in conjunction with his dealing with Baxter that he met her daughter Alice Baxter. It was with Alice that William ran off to Virginia—and took her mother along with them!

In Virginia William was involved in all sorts of legal activity. He was made constable of Fredrick County; then sued for unlawfully detaining a servant. He was selected as a juror but did not show up, so he was fined 400 pounds of tobacco. He was fined fifteen shillings for failure to keep his section of the road in repair, and he was charged as a breach of his constable duties and ordered to appear in court. He failed to appear, and the case was dismissed, however. He and Alice were sued by Patrick and Catherine Duncan for trespassing; they in turn sued the Duncans in 1755. Then in 1760 they were back in court on the same matter, but the lawsuit was "ordered to abate" since Patrick Duncan was dead.

The hottest legal activity involving William came after his death when his son Uriah challenged his deathbed will in which William had left his entire estate to his common-law wife, Alice Baxter "Duckworth." It became clear that Uriah and his mother Mary Wright Duckworth had won the estate when there appeared a notation that Uriah had sold the 235 Virginia acres which his father had purchased.

Alice Baxter "Duckworth" appeared back in court in 1763 on the trespassing issue and was awarded one hundred pounds. In a 1765 court appearance she was identified as the "Widow McGinn" but in 1796 her supposedly dead second husband was on the South Carolina census living alone with one slave.

In the 1790 Federal census for North Carolina, the "Widow McGinn" is listed as living as head of the household with three males over the age of sixteen and two female children. It is presumed that these children are children of William Duckworth.

3. George: Brother George did not live as colorful a life as his brother William. He married Jamima Williamson on June 26, 1739, and they lived in the Kingwood Township of New Jersey in 1778. They must have moved to Hunterdon County since the remainder of the information for George has him in that county. George was a witness for the will of Samuel Green of Amwell, Hunterdon County, New Jersey, in 1791, and he served in the Hunterdon County militia during the Revolutionary War.
[Source: Genealogy magazine of New York, Vol. 9, pp. 47-50)

4. Mary: Married Hugh Hartley on December 29, 1740, in Monmouth, New Jersey. They were assessed taxes for one cow on the 1768 Pennsylvania Tax and Exoneration and no other information was found. Mary died on September 15, 1746, in Burlington, New Jersey.

5. Joseph: Married Ester Ong on June 1, 1737, and they had at least four sons: William, Joseph M., Jeremiah, and "Captain" Jacob. Joseph Duckworth spent a lot of his time in court. He was found on court records for 1738, 1752, 1753, and 1754. He was in debt and was sued several times. In 1769 he served as a "chain man" on a survey for a land grant in Cumberland County, North Carolina. The land grant was for Joseph, Jr.

6. Anna: Was the youngest child of William and Grace Duckworth. She married Samuel Rose, a man of some prominence, in New Jersey. They had five children: Samuel, Martha, William, Thomas, and Ebenezer. Anna died on February 18, 1782, in Hopewell, Hunterdon County, New Jersey.

William Duckworth (Son of John and Sarah Hankins Duckworth and Grandson of William and Grace Cook Hunt)

William was born about 1735 in Frederick County, Virginia, and married Charity Jane (Unknown) of McDowell's Creek in Mecklenburg County, North Carolina. [Some information lists William's wife as Sarah Charity Rogers, but other sources cite Charity Jane with surname unknown.] John Duckworth bought 110 acres of land on McDowell's Creek, but it is unclear if this was William, his brother, or his son. At any rate, William moved onto this land in the late 1760s and established his home there.

William and Charity Jane were the parents of yet another John Duckworth, a Revolutionary War soldier and hero who settled in Burke County, North Carolina. John was severely wounded in the Battle of Ramseur's Mill but survived to fight in the Battle of Kings Mountain. He lived to be 83 years old.

Their first daughter was Althea Duckworth who probably married Sam Sherril, Jr., and moved to Blount County, Alabama, where she died.

William and Charity Jane named their next son William, who was born in 1765 and died in 1848 in Burke County, North Carolina. The next child was another daughter named, Sarah "Sallie" Duckworth, and she was born in 1765 on McDowell's Creek, Mecklenburg County, North Carolina, and died on February 6, 1840, in what became Buncombe County. She married David Robeson and they were the parents of nine children.

Another son was **Benjamin Duckworth,** born around 1765 on McDowell's Creek, North Carolina. [More information about Benjamin follows]. The next son born to William and Jane was Jonathan Duckworth, born about 1767 and died in November 1807 in Burke County, North Carolina. He married Kezziah England, the daughter of John and Jane Ann Grant England.

The last son was George Duckworth, born about 1771. He also served in the Revolutionary War and lived in Burke County, but he moved to McMinn County, Tennessee, where he died in 1841.

Benjamin Duckworth, Sr. (Son of William and Charity Jane Duckworth)

Benjamin Duckworth, Sr., married Mary Jolly sometime around 1791 also in North Carolina. There were twelve children born to this couple:

Mary, born 1784 in South Carolina, married Pryor Anderson, died sometime during 1793-1886 in South Carolina;

Elizabeth (1789 - 1898) married a Mr. Jolly;

Jacob, born between the years 1789 and 1815, married Frances E. __ and died before December 4, 1843;

Zabud, born April 28, 1792, in Anson County, North Carolina, married **Mary Jane (Polly) Thompson** in June 1819 in Pendleton District, South Carolina, and died on September 3, 1863, in Williamsburg, Covington County, Mississippi;

Joseph, born about 1800 in Pendleton District, South Carolina, married Mary (Polly) Green before 1825 [specific date unknown] in South Carolina, and died in 1872 in Smith County, Mississippi;

Sarah (Sally), born about 1802 in Pendleton District, South Carolina, married George W. Harper and Patrick C. Duckworth, died about 1880 near Sylvarena, Jones County, Mississippi;

Keziah, born January 4, 1806, in Anderson County (Pendleton District), South Carolina, married William Wages Speed, Jr., died May 5, 1886, in Williamsburg, Covington County, Mississippi;

Elnathan Daniel, born 1808 in Anderson County, South Carolina, married Mourning Garrison, and died between 1810 and 1899;

James Cooper, born a twin on December 20, 1811, in Anderson County, South Carolina, married Clary Ann Anderson before 1843 in South Carolina, and died before 1901;

Robert Crocker, born a twin on December 20, 1811, in Anderson County, South Carolina, married Elizabeth Wilson on October 25, 1832, in South Carolina, and died March 26, 1879, in Smith County, Mississippi;

Hester was born on August 6, 1814, in South Carolina, married Robert Guyton first and then married Col. J. L. Padget. She died July 23, 1889, in Smith County, Mississippi;

Charity was born on February 15, 1815, in Anderson County, South Carolina, married Zachariah T. Thompson, and died on October 30, 1869, in Jasper County, Mississippi.

There are a number of land transactions for Benjamin Duckworth in Anson County, North Carolina, and in the Pendleton District of upper South Carolina:

> Sometime during 1785-1799 he purchased 150 acres in Anson County, North Carolina, which had been part of a patent grant to Charles Lisenby. He sold this land in 1799. On May 24, 1797, he had surveyed a 200-acre tract which adjoined land he already owned, and he purchased additional land on February 24, 1797, in Anson County, which he then sold on January 22, 1800 (Anson County, North Carolina; Deed Book H2, pages 4-5).

[NOTE: It is also worth noting that the exact lines between North and South Carolina were often confused. In addition, the districts and counties in South Carolina were changed a number of times, and although the family might not have moved at all, the children were listed as having been born in different counties.]

In 1799 Benjamin purchased land in South Carolina even as he was buying and selling land in North Carolina, where he lived at the time. He bought 200 acres on Big Beaverdam Creek on Rocky River for $125 (Pendleton District, South Carolina: Deeds 1790-1806, p. 312). The deed was recorded on December 7, 1803. On August 15, 1800, he bought 85 acres on 26-Mile Creek of the Savannah River (Pendleton District, Deeds 1790-1806, p. 318) and on January 26, 1818, he sold land "on which Jacob Duckworth now lives." [He had a son by that name who lived in that area.] Benjamin's wife Mary is mentioned as having released her dower rights. Both signed by mark. (Anderson County, South Carolina; Deed Book O, p. 116) [Information from Anne Eiland. aeiland021@yahoo.com]

Sometime during the years of 1799 and 1800 Benjamin and Mary are found living in Pendleton District, South Carolina, where they are listed in the 1800 Census (on Page 30: five males, three females, and one slave). They appear in the 1810 Census again in Pendleton District with Ben, six males, seven females, and eight slaves. In 1820 Benjamin was still living in the Pendleton District, this time with five males, five females and seventeen slaves.

On November 25, 1825, Benjamin and Mary received a patent for 160 acres of Covington County land in Mississippi at approximately the present location of Old Hopewell Church and Hopewell Elementary School in what was to be known as the Hopewell Community in northeast Covington County. This was one of the earliest areas settled in the county (REF: T9N R15W Sec. 25, Cert. #698; Records of the General Land Office, National Archives, Washington, DC)

The tax rolls in Covington County show that the first members of the family to arrive in Mississippi were Benjamin's sons, Joseph (who first paid taxes on the 160 acres in the county in 1827) and Jacob (who paid taxes on 80 acres the same year). A George Duckworth, a William Duckworth, and an Obediah Duckworth had been in the county paying taxes from 1819, but it is unclear which land they were paying for.

Still in 1830, Benjamin Duckworth is listed in the Anderson County, South Carolina, Census. [Anderson County was a part of the Old Pendleton District.] At this time there were two males in the household in the 15-20 age range and one male in the 60-70 age range. There was one female 60-70 years of age and seventeen slaves.

Billy Paul Rogers of Collins, Mississippi, shared the following story:

> According to family tradition and hearsay handed down through the years, Benjamin Duckworth was 'a man of an enterprising disposition and the old home' was crowded, so he set out to look up a new country for himself and the households of his married children. He went to Tennessee, but did not like it there, so he went to Mississippi, where he ended up in northeast Covington County. He obtained land (Tract Book of 1819) and went back to report (to his family in South Carolina). He sent his son, Joseph Duckworth and family and some Negro slaves, out to settle the place and live there until he could come.

> When the family made the move, they came in a caravan of some 39 persons, including: '...He [unknown reference] married General Laurence's daughter of South Carolina, and their family, ...Monroe Speed, William and Benjamin. Afterwards, Big Ben Speed; their family; already mentioned Joseph Duckworth, who married Polly Green and their family; Crocker Duckworth, who married Lizzie Wilson and their family; Cooper Duckworth (a twin to Crocker) whose wife was General Garrison's daughter and

their family; Zabud Duckworth and his wife Polly Thompson and their family; Elnathan Duckworth, whose wife was General Garrison's daughter and their family; William Duckworth and Obediah Duckworth and their families; George Owenshad, who married widow Hathron and their family, Nick Hathornnis and his wife Betsy Bryant; Stockerly Turner and several young men came along with them, and they all settled in Covington County close around. And a thrifty, energetic lot of people they were, too.'

The men were good workers and careful to save what they made in the field and the country was fresh and stock of all kinds done well there but was very cheap, but the men saved money to buy Negro slaves with. The men that came here worked well and raised horses, cattle, hogs, and sheep, also grew corn, cotton, wheat, potatoes, peas, oats, and rice.

The women of the caravan of which I speak and their descendants were industrious and stout and made all or most of their clothing for these families, and that was before there were gins to separate the lint from the cotton seed. They would finger pick the cotton, then card and spin it into thread and then weave it into cloth. The cards, workbasket and spinning wheel were household necessities and it was a common thing for each of the families to have a share in the manufacturing of the cloth."

On February 15, 1834, Benjamin and his family joined the Leaf River Baptist Church, transferring their membership from Hopewell, South Carolina.

The 1840 Federal Census for Covington County, Mississippi, listed Benjamin Duckworth and his household, consisting of one male between the ages of 70 and 80 and one female between the ages of 60 and 70. They owned eleven slaves. Later in that year, Benjamin died in Moss Point, Mississippi, en route to Mobile, Alabama, to buy more slaves. His companions buried Benjamin in Moss Point.

Jacob Duckworth, the son of Benjamin and Mary, had died before his father, but his children [Frances E. Duckworth Smith and Samuel H. Duckworth] filed legal papers to get their share of their Grandfather Benjamin's estate. The signed and executed Memorandum of Settlement, dated August 29, 1838, from Smith County, Mississippi, seems to include only Benjamin's five heirs who were residents of that county. It is assumed that four other heirs, indicated as residents of Mississippi, were then living in nearby counties, likely Covington and Jones (REF: Photo prints of these family papers are in the Duckworth Collection, Barker Center, University of Texas).

Zabud Duckworth

Zabud Duckworth was the son of Benjamin Duckworth, Sr., and Mary Jolly. He was born on April 26, 1792, in the Anson District of North Carolina. His unusual given name has been spelled in a number of ways: Zarbud, Zabral, Zabard, Zabod, Zeabud, etc.

In June 1819 Zabud married Mary Jane (Polly) Thompson in the Pendleton District of South Carolina's "Up Country." She was born on February 5, 1803, in South Carolina, the daughter of Joseph Thompson and Mary (Molly) Jolly.

Zabud and Polly were part of the "Duckworth-Speed Caravan to Mississippi from South Carolina" led by Zabud's father, Benjamin Duckworth. They arrived in Covington County, Mississippi, sometime between 1820 and 1830. Of their fourteen children, eight married children of Meshack Rogers and two married Speed children:

George Benjamin, born in 1820 in Pendleton District, South Carolina, married Nancy Caroline Rogers, died in 1865 in Covington County, Mississippi, as a result of Civil War injuries;

Ellen, born October 18, 1822, in Pendleton District, South Carolina, married Benjamin Robert Speed, died December 21, 1896, in Fairfield, Freestone County, Texas;

Mary (Polly), born April 21, 1824, in Covington County, Mississippi, married Shadrack M. A. Rogers IV, died on January 22, 1884, in Oden, Montgomery County, Arkansas;

Sarah Elizabeth (Betsie), born October 20, 1825, in Covington County, Mississippi, married Timothy Luther Rogers, died August 13, 1864, in Covington County, Mississippi;

Kisiah (sometimes spelled Keziah), born November 1, 1827, in Pendleton District, South Carolina, married **Josiah Rogers**, died February 20, 1920, in Covington County, Mississippi;

Charity Pamelia, born April 19, 1828, married Benjamin Rawls, III, died on September 8, 1904, in Lamar County, Mississippi;

Frances Caroline, born December 25, 1830, in Covington County, Mississippi, married Marion Norvel Rogers, died October 17, 1861, in Covington County, Mississippi;

Joseph Thompson, born August 13, 1832, married Martha (Mary) Jane Speed, died March 4, 1887, in Ora, Covington County, Mississippi;

Daniel James Duckworth, born in 1834 in Covington County, Mississippi; and died about 1863 in a Civil War battle;

Hester Jane married George Benjamin Rogers first and then James Hill after Benjamin was killed in the Civil War. She was born on November 25, 1835, in Covington County and died on July 11, 1899, in Long Leaf, Louisiana;

Nancy Caroline was born July 17, 1837, in Covington County, Mississippi; married Meshack Rogers, Jr., died on December 28, 1937, in Collins, Covington County, Mississippi;

Rachel Rebecca was born on November 10, 1838, in Covington County, Mississippi, married her sister's widower, Timothy Luther Rogers, in 1866, and died on August 3, 1926, in Covington County;

Bronson (or Brunson) David was born on November 10, 1840, in Covington County, Mississippi, and died in a Civil War battle in Murfreesboro, Tennessee, on January 5, 1863;

Zabard F. Duckworth, Jr. was born in 1842 in Covington County, Mississippi, and died on September 23, 1864, in a Civil War battle near Barnesville, Lamar County, Georgia.

[NOTE: Kisiah Duckworth's brother, George Benjamin, was married to her sister-in-law, Nancy Caroline Rogers. So, he was her brother and her brother-in-law. Her sisters: Mary (Polly), Frances Caroline, Hester Jane, and Nancy Caroline Duckworth married her husband's brothers, so they were her sisters and her sisters-in-law. Kisiah's sisters, Sarah Elizabeth (Betsie) and Rachel Rebecca both married the same man, Timothy Luther Rogers, also a brother of Kisiah's husband.) Betsie died in 1864 in childbirth, and Rachel married Betsie's widower, Timothy Luther Rogers, in 1866.]

Zabud Duckworth bought 80 acres of land in Mississippi on September 28, 1836. On January 2, 1856, he purchased 40 acres and later bought another 40.38 acres.

He is listed as "Zeabud" on the U.S. Census for Covington County in 1840 as well as on the Mississippi State Census for 1841 and 1845. The 1850 Federal Census shows Zabud Duckworth in Covington County with a real estate valued at $350. Living with him was John F. Thompson, a teacher. In the 1860 Census, he is listed in Covington County and his real estate was valued at $3,000 with personal property valued at $21,000.

The November 13, 1847, "Minutes of the Leaf River [Baptist] Church," Covington County, Mississippi, states: "Indications of a work of grace in the congregation being visible on Sabbath (14) and Elders John P. Martin and John Moffete being in attendance, the church resolved to protract the meeting, which was accordingly continued until the 17th inclusive, during which time Zabud Duckworth and Mary Duckworth, his wife, (and) Elizabeth Speed were received by experience and baptized the 17th and in the afternoon."

The Civil War brought great personal tragedy to the Duckworth family. All five of the Duckworth sons fought in the war and four of them died, either being killed during the war or as a result of the war. Joseph Thompson was the only son to survive. Zabud himself died on September 3, 1863, and was buried in the Leaf River [Baptist Church] cemetery. His wife, Mary Jane (Polly) lived for twenty years after Zabud's death. She died on February 28, 1883, and was also buried in the Leaf River cemetery.

Kisiah Duckworth Rogers

Kisiah Duckworth was born on November 1, 1827, in the Washington District of South Carolina, which had been created in 1795 "to administer to the Up Country." Kisiah's parents, Zabud and Mary Jane (Polly) Thompson Duckworth actually lived in the portion of Washington District that was to become the Pendleton District in 1798.

On January 4, 1848, Kisiah married Josiah Rogers. They had twelve children, all of whom were born in Covington County, Mississippi:

Mary Malissa Rogers, born April 1849, married **J. King Byrd** in 1867, died April 21, 1921, in Mount Olive, Covington County, Mississippi;

Joseph Timothy Rogers, born April 4, 1850, married Mary Elizabeth (Molly) Thompson, died March 18, 1935, in Jasper County, Mississippi;

Benjamin Meshack Rogers, born March 21, 1851, married Ana Belle Yates, died on August 8, 1875, in Covington County, Mississippi;

Charity Elizabeth Rogers, born April 27, 1853, married Charles H. Colmer, died April 1922 in Forest County, Mississippi;

Daniel Caniday Rogers, born April 26, 1854, married Mary Alice "Mollie" Stamps, died April 11, 1938, in Salem, Covington County, Mississippi;

Zabud (or Zabard) Alonzo Rogers, born July 24, 1855, married three times: a) Mattie Walker-Hampton, b) Sarah M. Byrd (daughter of J. King Byrd and step-daughter of his wife, Mary Malissa Rogers Byrd), and c) Margaret Janie Boswick, died November 20, 1929, in Covington County, Mississippi;

Arthur Lafayette Rogers, born April 8, 1857, married Sarah Amanda Barnes, died on July 3, 1909, in Covington County, Mississippi;

Josiah Brunson Rogers, born June 10, 1858, married Maybelle "Mable" Stamps, died on December 8, 1935, in Lawrence County, Mississippi;

Lucy Kisiah Rogers, born September 27, 1859, married Duncan C. Buchanan, died July 18, 1921, Covington County, Mississippi;

Absalom Columbus Rogers, born January 29, 1861, married Sarah Elizabeth Dixon, died August 4, 1893, in Covington County, Mississippi;

Norvel Dolberry Rogers, born May 14, 1862, married Susie Matilda Holder, died August 7, 1944, in Jasper Co., Mississippi;

John William Rogers, born August 16, 1864, married Anna Kate Holloway, died December 31, 1935, in Forest County, Mississippi

Kin

Kisiah was widowed in 1864 when Josiah Rogers returned home, wounded, from a Civil War battle. He died shortly after arriving home. She continued to live on their farm, raising eleven children by herself, but by the 1900 Census, Kisiah had moved in with her youngest son, John W. Rogers, and his wife Kate, and by 1910, she had moved in with her son, Zabud ("Zake").

Kisiah died on February 10, 1910, at the age of 83. She had been a widow for 46 years. There were two obituaries for Kisiah, the first written by N. R. Stone, her pastor at Rock Hill Baptist Church and the second one was carried in the county newspaper under the heading, "Noble Mother Gone."

> On November 1, 1827, God gave to Mr. and Mrs. Zarbard Duckworth of South Carolina a jewel of the rarest hue. Early in life this daughter was brought to Mississippi.
>
> On January 4, 1848, she was married to Josiah Rogers. To this union God gave nine sons and three daughters. From a wound received during the Civil War, Mr. Rogers was laid to rest with the Boys in Gray thus leaving her to brave the dangers and undergo the difficulties of widow and orphan. But the difficulties were met and overcome. Today all except two boys await the call to which Mother answered February 20, 1910, as noble a body of high-toned Christian citizens as this country affords. All members of a Baptist church and four of the men are deacons. This is but the result of over sixty years of faithful service in the Kingdom of God.
>
> Mrs. Rogers' memorial cannot be obtained by pen, tongue or brush, but abides in the lives blessed by her kind words, golden deeds, untiring energy and Motherly influence. May God give to this world more such mothers in Israel.
>
> On February the 21st amid sobs and sighs of a tremendous congregation, she was laid to rest in Rock Hill cemetery. Peace to her memory until the angels awake her in the morning of the resurrection.
> ***********
>
> Mrs. Keziah Rogers was born in South Carolina, November 1st, 1827. She came with her father, Zabral Duckworth, to Mississippi when quite a child.

72

She was married to Josiah Rogers, January 4th, 1848. To them were born nine sons and three daughters. All the children grew to manhood and woman-hood. Seven sons and three daughters survive her.

In the death of Mrs. Rogers, the community gives up one of the noble women and one of the best mothers the county has ever known. She was an earnest Christian, having been a member of the [Rock Hill] Baptist Church for sixty years. Her husband gave his life to his country, dying of a wound received in the Civil War. Some estimate of her life may be realized when we think how she provided for her large family of children and reared them in such a way that it was even a marvel to her neighbors.

Her children have all made high-toned Christian characters. They stand among the foremost citizens in the communities where they live and can always be found ready to stand on the right side of every moral question. Four of her sons are deacons in Baptist churches. She indeed fought a good fight and has now gone to her reward.

Mary Malissa Rogers

The first child and daughter of Josiah Rogers and Kisiah Duckworth Rogers was **Mary Malissa Rogers**, born in April 12, 1849. After her father's death from Civil War injuries, Malissa helped her mother care for the younger children and the home and farm. [More information about Malissa Rogers Byrd can be found in *Traveling Companions*, another book by this author.]

In 1869 she married John King Byrd, who was seventeen years her senior. They were the parents of eight children, the first son being James Edward Byrd, the grandfather of Hersey Davis Byrd.

Kisiah Duckworth, through her daughter, Mary Malissa Rogers Byrd, is the link between the Duckworth family and the Byrd family.

Sources:

Byrd Family History
Family Notes by Valois Byrd
Church History, Rock Hill Baptist Church
Personal Visits
Internet:
  Ancestry.com
  Geni.com: /people/Benjamin-Duckworth/6000000003538708961
  Genealogy.com
  Genealogy Trails.com
  Mitchellfarms.com
  Roster of 46th Mississippi Infantry, Company B, Civil War
  FamilySearch.com
Rodgers-Rogers: Westward from the Carolinas by William Morgan Brown
  (Decorah, Iowa: Anundsen Publishing Company, 1996)
History of Anson County, North Carolina, 175-1976 by Mary L. Medley
  (Charlotte, N. C.: Heritage Printers, Inc., 1976)
Anne Eiland, Scottsdale, Arizona: Aeiland0218@yahoo.com

Kay Byrd

THE EARGLE FAMILY

How does the Eargle family relate to the Byrd family?

Christian (or Christina) Eargle married James McNure. Their son was Henry Adam David McNure, who changed his name after the Civil War to McNeil. David McNeil's daughter, Effie Leona McNeil, married James Edward Byrd, the grandfather of Hersey Davis Byrd.

There is a small mountain range covering parts of southern Germany, Switzerland, and France called the Jura Mountains. In these mountains is a valley known during the 10th and 11th centuries, and possibly even later than that, as the Erguel Valley. No one knows for sure why this valley was so named, but it is supposed that a family of the same name settled in this area and built a castle-fortress, the remains of which are still visible today. The castle was named Chateau d'Erguel, but is known today as Vallon de St. Imier and is a Swiss tourist attraction.

Dolan Hoye Eargle, Jr., wrote on a message board on www.ancestry.com that he had actually visited the Chateau d'Erguel. He writes: "It commands a height in a valley...and was one of a chain of round communication towers in Switzerland" all along the Rhone River. He goes on to explain that at some point the castle was controlled by a duke from the neighboring French Burgundy region, but it was basically destroyed during the Thirty Years' War. Some researchers believe that the immigrants bearing the name of Ergle or Eargle were originally from this region.

In addition to the Thirty Years' War in Europe, other wars impacted the lives of the Eargle family. The destruction of the land, the poor economy, the lack of religious freedom, and the conscription of young men pulled into military service resulted in unrest and the dissatisfaction of this family and other residents of the area.

Later, in America, the French and Indian War [known in Europe as the Seven Years' War] impacted Europeans as well.

> In the New World, Charles Town in the Province of Carolina had been settled in 1670 and was thriving as a port, but during the 1700s the citizens in town and the plantation owners in the surrounding areas (called the Low Country) were besieged by Indians who were aided and abetted by the French as a part of the French and Indian War. To quell the attacks and ensure settlement of unused land, King George II of England (a German

native himself) offered bounty land grants to any German who would be willing to relocate to America.
[Source: Wikipedia "The Thirty Years' War]

The King George land grants required that anyone who received a land grant would cultivate the land, build dwellings, and defend their property against the French-incited Indians. This would protect the City of Charleston and other low country dwellings.

Immigrants left their homes and traveled the long distance to the Rhine River and down the Rhine to the Port of Rotterdam, bringing food and a few of their personal belongings. After a stay of possibly as long as several weeks in Rotterdam, the ship sailed and stopped briefly in Portsmouth, England, to take on provisions for the long voyage across the Atlantic to America. Some were able to pay for their passage and others served as indentured servants to pay for their passage. Accommodations aboard the ship were sparse, with families sometimes sharing a single bunk in crowded quarters, taking turns sleeping. Food and water were rationed carefully to provide for the long journey.
[Source:familytreemaker.genealogy.com/users/s/h/e/Lavanda_N_Se llnut/GENE2-0014.html]

The Eargle family could have been in one of these groups to leave German soil, or they could have come from the Erguel Valley in Switzerland. They were a German-speaking family, so they could have originated in either country.

Johan Michale Eargle (or Ergle), along with his children, Mary Eve, 24; Johan Michale, age 22; and Michael, age 13, boarded the *Upton* in Rotterdam and made the long voyage across the Atlantic, arriving in Charles Town harbor on September 12, 1752. As luck would have it, the passengers faired quite well on the oceanic journey but were caught in a horrendous hurricane in the Charles Town harbor.

The *Upton*, a 180-ton ship, was built in Baltimore and registered on November 9, 1749, and known as a 'pink' or 'pinkie,' with both the bow and the stern shaped in a point, the traditional shape of ships built up to about 1750. It was later registered in Liverpool and under contract to the firm of Austin and Laurens, Attorneys, of Charles Town.

Kay Byrd

The Internet author quoted above also located several newspaper articles related to the hurricane and its effects on the ship and its passengers:

1. A ship is just arrived from Rotterdam with German Servents [sic] in perfect Health (not one of them having died in passage). Amongst them are Tradesmen of all sorts which will be indented [sic] on very reasonable terms.
[Source: Austin & Laurens, *South Carolina Gazette*, September 19, 1752]

2. On the 14th in the evening, it began to blow very hard, the wind being a NE and the sky looked wild and threatening. It continued blowing from the same point, till about 4 o'clock in the morning of the 15th, at which time it became more violent and rained, increasing very fast till about 9, when the flood came in like a bore, filling the harbor in a few minutes. Before 11 o'clock, all the vessels in the harbor were on shore, except *The Hornet*, a Man-o-War, which rode it out by cutting away her mainmast; all wharfs and bridges were ruined, and every house and store upon them beaten down and carried away, with all the goods therein, as were many houses in the town, and abundances of roofs, chimneys, etc., almost all the tile or slated houses were uncovered and great quantities of merchandize, etc., in the stores on the bay street damaged by their doors being burst open.
[Source: *South Carolina Gazette*, September 19, 1752]

3. A notice in one Charles Town newspaper noted "streets overflowed, the tide at sea having rose upwards of ten feet about the high water mark at spring-tides, and nothing now to be seen but ruins of houses, canoes, wrecks of boats, masts, yards, incredible quantities of all sorts of timber, barrels, staves, shingles, household and other goods floating and driving with great violence through the streets and round about the town. The inhabitants, finding themselves in the midst of a tempestuous sea, the wind still continuing, the tide (according to its common course) being expected to flow till after one o'clock and many of the people being already up to their necks in water in their houses, began now to think of nothing but

certain death. But (here we must record as signal, an instance of the immediate disposition of the Divine Providence as ever appeared) they were soon relieved from their apprehensions; for about 10 minutes after 11 o'clock the wind veered to the ESE and SW very quick, and then, tho' it continued its violence and the sea beat and dashed everywhere in amazing impetuosity, there was a sudden fall, or every house and inhabitant in this town, must, in all probability have perished, and before 3 o'clock the hurricane was entirely over. Many people were drowned, and others much hurt by the fall of houses...

...the ship *Upton*, of Liverpoole, lately arrived from Rotterdam which lay up Ashley River, was drove a great way into the marsh near Wappoo.

...for about 30 miles round Charles Town there is hardly a plantation that has not lost every outhouse upon it. All our roads are so fill'd with trees blown down and broke down, that traveling is rendered extremely difficult. "[Source: *South Carolina Gazette*]

4. *The Charles-Town Mercury* related: "A ship with a cargo of Palatines (*The Upton*) anchored in the Ashley River was with anchors driven on the marsh near James Island where she tossed so violently as to cause the death of twelve of them."

5. Advertisement in the *South Carolina Gazette*, Charles-Town, October 30, 1752: "Whereas the ship UPTON, Captain Gardiner, has been driven upon a marsh near Wappon Creek by late storm, and it will be necessary that a channel be dug through the marsh of 80 or 100 feet long and about 35 feet wide, and 5 or 6 feet deep. Any person both able and willing to undertake such a business, are desired to offer their proposals to Austin and Laurens."

6. Notice in the *South Carolina Gazette*: "Ship Departures, February 12, 1753, Ship UPTON, John Gardiner, to Maryland."

John Michael Eargle, Sr.

After weeks at sea, it must have been traumatic for the Eargle family to endure this mighty hurricane. Soon after landing, however, on October 3,

Kay Byrd

1752, Johan Michal Eargle [now known as John Michael Eargle, Sr.] applied for and received a "bounty land grant" on the Wateree Creek near St. Jacob's Lutheran Church, Chapin, South Carolina. It was granted on "23rd November 1754." He and his "heirs and assigns" were given "a Plantation or tract of land measuring two hundred and fifty acres situate lying and being in the fork between the Broad and Saludy Rivers, butting and bounding to the northward part on vacant land and part on land laid out unto Christian Theus and on all other sides by land not laid out." [Source: Ancestry.com Land Grant for John Mich. Ergle]

The Grant further states: "And hath such shape, form and marks, as appears by a plat there, hereunto annexed: Together with all woods, under-woods, timber and timber trees, lakes, ponds, fishings, waters, water courses, profits, commodities, appurtances [sic] and hereditaments [sic] whatsoever, thereunto belonging or in any wise appertaining: Together with privilege of hunting, hawking, fowling in and upon the same, and all mines and minerals whatsoever; saving and reserving, nevertheless, to us, our heirs and successors, all white pine trees, if any there should be found growing thereon; and also saving and reserving, to us, and successors, one-tenth part of mines of silver and gold only: TO HAVE AND TO HOLD, the said tract of Two hundred and fifty acres of land and all and singular other the premises hereby granted with the appurtances, unto the said John Michael Ergil, his Heirs and assigns forever...

The newly arrived Eargles "settled in the Wateree Creek area of the Dutch Fork" which lies at the confluence of the Broad and Saluda Rivers in the old "royal" Colleton County of South Carolina. [This county became the Lexington District in 1804, not to be confused with present-day City of Lexington, South Carolina.] It appears that the land grant was near Chapin, South Carolina. Inserted below is a brief history of the town of Chapin:

In the mid-1700s, when everything west of Columbia was frontier, a group of German settlers, many of them armed with land grants from the English crown, laid claim to the land between the forks of the Saluda and Broad Rivers. It came to be known as the Dutch Fork, the "Dutch" being an anglicized form of Deutsch (referring to the German language and people).

Few of the Fork's German settlers ever left its boundaries, and even fewer outsiders ever came to stay. In the 1800's, Dutch

79

Forkers had developed their own subculture, their own particular—some would say peculiar—ways. Some still spoke German well into the 19th century, and those who didn't, had a dialect all their own. They measured success not in money or fame, but in family and community ties. They were poor, but proud. They made the most of the little they had. They believed in hard work, in saving up for even harder times, and in a benevolent God...

Martin Chapin was the town [of Chapin]'s founder and the area became known for its timber. It was not until the advent of the automobile, electricity, the telephone and the radio that the Dutch Fork area was opened up to the outside world.

But nothing could have prepared these poor folks, who had lived and worked the land along the banks of the Saluda River for years, for the tremendous social upheaval that resulted from the damming of the Saluda River in 1927 to create Lake Murray...

The lives of some 5,000 people were directly affected as land was acquired. Three churches, six schools, and 193 graveyards were removed. To some, the building of the dam brought employment. New people moved in. New students from other sections of the country were welcomed into the schools. A new age had begun. For others, only memories remained of the lives they had known. For quite a few, the adjustment was impossible...

Many of the land grant homes that had been built in the 1700s and 1800s ended up under Lake Murray, including some burial sites of earlier settlers.
[Source: https://www.chapinsc.com/173/A-History-of-Chapin]

[Note: There are many, many Eargle family trees on the Internet and each one is different. Since choosing the right genealogy is basically a "stab in the dark," the information and genealogy that follow is from a website called "Dutch Fork Chapter.Org" and is presumably the work of the Aiken County, South Carolina, Historical Commission.

There is a log cabin in Aiken, South Carolina, called the Frederick Ergle Log Cabin. It was built in 1808 and a plaque says, "A sesquicentennial memorial gift to the City of Aiken by the family of Thomas H. Williamson

(1888-1962) Former County Treasurer, Member of Aiken County Historical Commission and Direct Descendent of this cabin's builder. This is a related family to the John Michael Ergil family.]

There seems to be disagreement as to whether or not John Eargle's wife accompanied him and the children to Charles Town. Some records indicate there was no mention of a wife, while others list Anna Maria "Mary" [born in 1705] as his wife. Still other family trees list Catherine Freshley as the wife of John Michael Eargle, Sr., although others list Catherine Freshley as the wife of his son. According to one note on Ancestry.com, the Upton passenger list identifies his wife as "Anna," age 46. There is further speculation that his wife was killed in the hurricane when it hit their ship in the Charles Town Harbor. (Source: VickiNicholson52@Ancestry.com/mediaui-viewer/tree...]

With or without his wife, John Michael Eargle, Sr., worked the land and lived on the property in Dutch Fork until his death in 1786. Upon his death, John Michael, Jr., inherited the property by the law of primogeniture.

John Michael Eargle, Jr.

As stated previously Michael, Jr., came to America with his father and siblings in 1752. With his family he lived on the land granted by King George II and may have married Catherine Freshley. He fathered a number of children and died around 1797. [Some family trees suggest he died "before 1773."]

Children of John Michael Eargle, Jr. were:

John Jacob Ergle was probably born around 1774 in the Lexington District of South Carolina, married Rebecca Schaffer first and then Mary Magdalene "Polly" Amick. He died in 1837.

Michael Eargle was born about 1774, married Anna Barbara Wessinger, and died in 1818. [More information on Michael follows.]

Barbara Eargle, born on April 16, 1773, married a Mr. Huitt, and died on November 20, 1853.

Eve Eargle died on January 10, 1843. The date of her birth is unknown.

Michael Eargle

This Michael Eargle (1774-1818) was probably named for his uncle Michael who arrived in South Carolina in 1752 from Germany. It is assumed that the children and grandchildren of John Michael Eargle, Sr., all lived on the land grant in the Lexington District of South Carolina, although records indicate that in 1816 Michael Eargle bought 500 acres on Bear Creek from Edmund Bellinger.
[Source: www.dutchfordchapter.org]

Michael married Anna Barbara Wessinger, the daughter of Matthias Wessinger, Sr., and Lydia Ann Smith. The Wessingers had also come from Germany and settled in the general area. To this union were born several children:

Nancy Eargle was born about 1802, married John Slice, the son of Uriah Slice and the brother of Elias Slice, and died in July 1896.

Margaret Catherine Eargle was born on September 28, 1802. She married Joshua Taylor (1809-1880), the son of Jonathan Taylor and Rachel Clark, on February 5, 1837. Margaret died on October 29, 1886, and is buried alongside her husband in the Boiling Springs Methodist Church Cemetery in Lexington County, South Carolina.

Mary Magdalena Eargle was born about 1803 and married Elias Slice, the brother of her sister's husband.

Rebecca Eargle was born in 1810 and married David Derrick, the son of Andrew Derrick and Catherine Hiller. Rebecca and David Derrick are buried in the Derrick Cemetery, Lake Murray.

Christian (sometimes spelled Christina) Eargle was born about 1811 and married James McNure, born about 1803. [More about this person follows.]

David Eargle was born in 1814 and married Mary Magdalene Wessinger, the daughter of Uriah Wessinger and Elizabeth Derrick. He died about 1850.

Sally Eargle, born about 1816, married Jeremiah "Jesse" Miller, the son of Henry Mill and Permelia Taylor. She died on December 12, 1876.

Mary Barbara Eargle, born about 1817, married Levi Shealy on December 7, 1837. He was born on April 14, 1816, and was the son of John Ventle Shealy and Eva Margaret Sease.

Michael Eargle died in 1818, and his will was probated with Uriah Wessinger and Isaac Lybrand as administrators. Of the 500 acres he bought on Bear Creek, 179 acres were taken as dower rights by his widow, Barbara Eargle, which the heirs sold in 1845 to David Derrick, his son-in-law, following the death of Barbara.
[Source: B. H. Holcomb, "Memorialized Records of Lexington District, South Carolina, 1814-1825 at www.dutchforkchapter.org_and_Lexington Deed O-129]

Christian (or Christina) Eargle

Christian married James McNure who was born in Columbia, South Carolina, which was established as the state capital of South Carolina in 1786. They lived in the old Lexington District of South Carolina and are mentioned in the 1840 and 1850 U.S. Federal Census as residents of the County of Lexington, South Carolina. They had five children:

Martha E. McNure was born in 1839 in Lexington District, South Carolina. She married Henry Anderson Smith, and they had at least one son, David Monroe Smith;

Henry Adam David McNure was born on November 27, 1841. [More information about David follows];

Mary McNure was born in 1843;

George W. McNure was born in 1845 and died on April 4, 1909. He served in the Civil War from Mississippi and married after the war was over. He is buried in Beauvoir Confederate Cemetery in Biloxi, Mississippi;

Louisa "Lou" McNure was born in 1849.

Christian and James, with all their children, moved to Mississippi some time before 1866. They are listed in the Mississippi State Census in 1866 and in the Federal Census in 1870 as residents of Smith County, Mississippi. Since both sons enlisted in the Confederate Army from Mississippi, it would seem that the McNures moved some time prior to 1861.

The dates of the deaths of Christian and James are unknown, but it is assumed that both are buried in Mississippi.

Henry Adam David McNure

After the Civil War, David McNure changed his surname to McNeil in honor of his commanding officer during the war. He married Sarah Caroline McLaurin on November 30, 1871, in Simpson County, Mississippi, where they made their home in the Jaynesville community.

Following the stillborn birth of a daughter in 1873, David and Caroline welcomed to the world another daughter whom they named **Effie Leona McNeil**. Leona was born on April 6, 1877, and was a dutiful daughter to her parents. Another daughter was stillborn and then their son, Hugh Alexander McNeil, was born on March 19, 1883. They had no other children.

In the 1870 Federal Census, David McNeil is listed as a farmer, owning 800 acres. His wife Caroline was a homemaker. The entire family were active in the Hopewell Presbyterian Church. David served as an elder and both children were baptized there.

Sarah Caroline died on January 6, 1916, and David died on March 20, 1924. Both are buried in the cemetery of Hopewell Presbyterian Church in Simpson County, Mississippi.

Effie Leona McNeil

After completing college and teaching school in Bassville, Mississippi, Leona married James Edward Byrd on May 10, 1898, at her parents' home in Jaynesville, Mississippi. The newlyweds made their home in Mt. Olive, Covington County, Mississippi, and were the parents of seven children: Melissa Corrine "Connie" Byrd (1901-1992); Juanita Caroline Byrd Huang

(1904-1988); Annie Ward Byrd (1907-2000); Mary Hasseltine Byrd Ball (1909-1990); Edward Leavell Byrd (1912-2004); Hugh McNeil Byrd (1914-2002); and Leona Valois Byrd (1918-2001). [A complete story about Leona McNeil Byrd, James Edward Byrd, and each of the seven siblings can be found in two books by this author: *Traveling Companions* and *Oaks of Righteousness.*]

Christian Eargle McNure is the link between the Eargle family and the Byrd family and through her descendants (David McNure/McNeil, Effie Leona McNeil Byrd, Edward Leavell Byrd) to Hersey Davis Byrd.

Sources:

Wikipedia: "Chateau d'Erguel," and the Thirty Years' War.
Familytreemarker.genealogy.com/users/s/h/e/Lavanda_N_Sellnut/GENE2-0014.html.
South Carolina Gazette, September 19, 1752 and February 12, 1753.
Google.com: "A History of Chapin."
Ancestry.com
    Land Grant for John Mich. Ergle
    VickiNicholson52@Ancestry.com/mediaui-viewer/tree...]
B. H. Holcomb, "Memorialized Records of Lexington District, South Carolina, 1814-1825."
www.dutchforkchapter.org
Family stories and on-site visits, personal observations.

THE JOLLY FAMILY

How does the Jolly family relate to the Byrd family?

Mary "Polly" Jolly married Benjamin Duckworth, and their son Zabud Duckworth had a daughter named Kisiah Duckworth. Kisiah married Josiah Rogers whose daughter was Mary Malissa Rogers and she married John King Byrd. Mary Malissa Rogers became the mother of James Edward Byrd. J. E. Byrd's son was Edward Leavell Byrd and his grandson is Hersey Davis Byrd.

The Jolly family originated in England under the various spellings of the name: Jolliffe, Jolli, Jollye, Joulee, and so forth. It was thought to be of Norman origin, derived from the Norman word *joli*, meaning jolly or merry.

According to the website, houseofnames.com, the first family using this name was found in Staffordshire, England, "where they were an ancient family granted lands by William the Conqueror." The family had "enjoyed power and affluence in Europe before the Norman Conquest." Many amateur genealogists trace their lineage back to this family in England. [Source: https://www.houseofnames.com/jolliffe-family-crest]

Due to the political and religious unrest of the 17th century and the lure of America's vast resources, several Jolliffe men emigrated to the New World. In America, their surname was changed to Jolly.

Researchers cite John Jolliffe, who was born in Cofton Hackett, Worcestershire, England on May 28, 1641, as their Jolliffe ancestor. He was the son of Thomas Jolliffe, Esquire, and Margaret Skinner, and he married Mary Rigglesworth. He and his wife came to America in 1652 and lived in the Norfolk, Virginia, area, where he died on November 28, 1716. He fathered eight children, among whom were Thomas Jolliffe (1671-1736) and John Joliffe (1665-1736). It has been difficult to find a link between this John Jolliffe family and the ancestors from South Carolina, however.

The "backcountry" in South Carolina, namely the Ninety-Six District, had three Jolly men listed in their 1799 census: Joseph, James, and William. It is possible one, or all, of these men ventured south from Virginia by way of North Carolina and settled in the huge Ninety-Six District, but the relationship between these men and with John Jolliffe in Virginia is uncertain.

[Note: The term "backcountry" was used in South Carolina to distinguish it from the more prominent "low country" of southern South Carolina around the Charleston area. After the Revolutionary War, "backcountry" became known as the "upcountry," but still distinguishing it from Charleston's high society.]

The Jolly men were active in the Revolutionary War in South Carolina. In his book, *The Hornet's Nest*, Jimmy Carter identifies these men and their neighbors as "The Over Mountain rebels." He says:

> [They] were fiercely independent pioneers, unwilling to accept any restraints on their personal freedom. They were creatures of the woods and hills, and more familiar with aiming their rifles at bear, deer, and turkey than at other men. Their first inclination had been to remain aloof from the mounting conflict between Whigs and Tories, but...as Cornwallis began to expand control of western Carolina, they had to consider how best to respond to the eastern, or 'flatlands,' conflict. They were determined that the Redcoats would not control their region and were pleased" [to join forces with rebels from Georgia.]

The Over Mountain boys included the following men from the Jolly family:

Joseph Jolly was a Captain in the Revolutionary War and served under Colonel John Thomas. He was in the expedition against Indians and in the Florida Expedition during 1778.

Wilson Jolly was also in the Revolutionary War.

Benjamin Jolly was a Lieutenant under Captain Palmer in 1779 and a Captain under Colonel Thomas Brandon in 1781. He served as a Major under Colonel Farr in the Battle of Cowpens.

James Jolly served in the militia under Captain Benjamin Jolly and Colonel Thomas Brandon. He served from May 7, 1780, until June 25, 1781.

John Jolly enlisted in 1776 and served under Captain Joseph Jolly and Colonel John Thomas against the Indians. He was also in the Florida Expedition in 1778 as a Lieutenant under Colonel Thomas Brandon and in the Stono Campaign near Charleston.

In May 1781 he was killed by Tories at "Leighton's" near Fair Forest Creek in the Ninety-Six District of upper South Carolina.

[NOTE: The   Battle   of **Stono** Ferry   was   an American Revolutionary War battle, fought on June 20, 1779, near Charleston, South Carolina.
Source: https://en.wikipedia.org/wiki/Battle_of_Stono_Ferry]

Joseph Jolly, Sr.

An online researcher, Thelma Prince, lists many, many legal transactions for Joseph Jolly, Sr., in Ninety-Six District of South Carolina. She also assumes that his sons were William and Joseph Jolly, Jr. In addition, she notes that a James Jolly and a Wilson Jolly also appear in land transactions.
[Source: Ancestry.com: Posted 6 Jun 2008 by grjolly1 and written by Thelma Faye Cain Prince]

Joseph Jolley lived in the Ninety-Six District from 1771 until 1788. He married Mary Brockington (1721-1760) and they settled on the Thickity Creek in the Ninety-Six District. Some researchers speculate that this Joseph Jolly was the son of Thomas Jolliffe and his wife, Mary Bishop, from the Norfolk, Virginia, area.

Joseph Jolley held 600 acres of land, recorded in Mecklenburg County, North Carolina, but the state and county lines were blurred in those early days and his land might have actually been in the Ninety-Six District of South Carolina.
[Source: Ancestry.com: Joseph Jolly]

[Note: The old Ninety-Six District of South Carolina was a political and military designation from early days until 1785 when the South Carolina legislature tried to divide the Province of South Carolina into counties. It remained the Ninety-Six District until 1800, but the counties of Spartanburg, Union, Laurens, Newberry, Abbeville, and Edgefield were actually designated counties within the Ninety-Six District in 1785. After the Revolutionary War, Greenville and Pendleton Counties were added. In 1800 the Ninety-Six District was abolished. In 1826 the Pendleton District was divided into Pickens and Anderson counties. After the Civil War, in 1868, all districts became counties.]

William Jolly

If Thelma Prince [cited above] is correct, William Jolly was the son of Joseph Jolly, Sr. He married Frances Herring and they had a number of children.

James Lewis Jolly, Sr., (a twin to Joseph Jolley) was born on February 22, 1768, in the old Ninety-Six District, South Carolina; died in 1830 in the same area;

Joseph Jolly, born on February 22, 1768, in the old Ninety-Six District; died on November 2, 1807, in what was then designated as Pendleton District, Anderson County, South Carolina;

Mary Jane Jolly, born in 1771 in the Ninety-Six District, South Carolina; married Benjamin Case Duckworth, and died in 1860 in Covington County, Mississippi [Inserted by this author];

John Bradley Jolly, born in 1776 in the old Ninety-Six District of South Carolina; date of death unknown;

Jesse Jolly, born sometime between 1776 and 1794 in the old Ninety-six District of South Carolina; died in 1830 in Franklin County, Georgia;

Patsey Jolly Hunnicutt, born in 1780 in the old Ninety-Six District; died in Headstone, South Carolina;

Maxey (or Mansey) Jolly, born on September 10, 1780, in the old Ninety-six District; married Nancy Price in 1805 in Pendleton District, South Carolina; died on May 20, 1857, in Posey County, Indiana;

William Jolly, born 1782 in old Ninety-Six District, South Carolina and died in the same area although the date of his death is unknown;

Eleanor Jolly, born in 1784 in South Carolina; no further information is known.
[Source: ancestry.com: mediaui-viewer/tree]

[Note: Although William and Frances Herring Jolly had a number of children and one of them was named "Mary Jane," it is not clear if this

Mary Jane was the person who married Benjamin Duckworth. The dates of their Mary Jane, 1771-1860, match Mary Jolly Duckworth, however. The information was inserted in the above list as an assumption, is purely speculative, and has not been sufficiently documented. A lot of amateur genealogists have offered various family members, ancestors, and descendants for the Jolly family. This information is at best an educated guess. Records for the backcountry (or upcountry) of South Carolina are old and many have been destroyed, so it is necessary to use whatever records are available and to surmise who the ancestors might have been.]

William and Frances Jolly moved to Franklin County, Georgia, along with other family members, and William died there around 1831. His will was probated in Franklin County, Georgia, as well as in Pendleton District, South Carolina.

Benjamin Case Duckworth did, in fact, marry Mary "Polly" Jolly, and they were the parents of the following children, all of whom were born in the Carolinas:

> Mary Duckworth, born 1784, married Pryor Anderson; died sometime before 1886;
>
> Elizabeth Duckworth, born between the years 1789 and 1815 and died sometime before 1898;
>
> Jacob Duckworth, born between 1789 and 1815, and died before December 4, 1843 in Harris County, Texas;
>
> **Zabud (or Zabard) Duckworth**, born April 28, 1792, married Mary Jane "Polly" Thompson in June 1819; and died on September 3, 1863 in Williamsburg, Covington County, Mississippi;
>
> Joseph Duckworth, born about 1800, married Mary "Polly" Green; and died in 1872 in Smith County, Mississippi;
>
> Sarah "Sally" Duckworth, born 1802, married George W. Harper first and then Patrick C. Duckworth; died 1880 in Jones County, Mississippi;

Keziah Catherine "Kid" Duckworth, born January 4, 1806, married William Wages Speed, Jr., on October 18, 1821; died on May 5, 1886 in Williamsburg, Covington County, Mississippi;

Elnathan Daniel Duckworth, born on February 4, 1808, married Mourning Garrison first and then Anna S. Garrison. He died on May 8, 1883, in Bastrop, Morehouse Parish, Louisiana;

James Cooper Duckworth, born December 20, 1811, married Clary Ann Anderson, and died on May 12, 1866, in Morehouse Parish, Louisiana;

Robert Crocker Duckworth, born December 20, 1811, married Elizabeth Wilson on October 25, 1832, and died on March 26, 1879, in Smith County, Mississippi;

Hester O. Duckworth was born on August 6, 1814, in Anderson County, South Carolina, and first married Robert Guyton, the father of her five children. In later years she married Col. J. L. Padget with whom she moved to Mississippi. Hester died July 23, 1889, in Smith County, Mississippi;

Charity Duckworth, born February 15, 1815, married Zachariah T. Thompson, died October 30, 1869, in Jasper County, Mississippi.

The family moved to Mississippi, almost *en masse*, in a wagon train (or caravan) and settled in the new County of Covington in the State of Mississippi. Benjamin and Polly had been members of a Baptist church in South Carolina and moved their membership to the Leaf River Baptist Church in the Williamsburg area. They purchased a great many acres in the area and established a home near kin and friends from South Carolina. [Note: More information on Benjamin and Polly can be found in the chapter entitled The Duckworth Family.]

In 1840, Benjamin died while on a trip to Mobile to purchase slaves. His companions buried him in Moss Point, Mississippi. Mary "Polly" Duckworth outlived her husband by twenty years and died in 1860. She was buried in the Leaf River Baptist Church cemetery, Covington County, Mississippi.

Suffice it to say that the ancestors of Mary "Polly" Jolly Duckworth are an unsolved mystery, especially to this writer. The Jolly family were outstanding patriots and early settlers in an untamed part of South Carolina, and their descendants paved the way for settlement in the western lands of Mississippi.

The link between the Jolly family and the Byrd family is with Mary Jolly Duckworth and through her descendants (Zabud Duckworth, Kisiah Duckworth, Mary Malissa Rogers Byrd, James Edward Byrd, Edward Leavell Byrd) to Hersey Davis Byrd.

Sources:

www.houseofnames.com/jolliffe-family-crest
www.ancestry.com: Posted 6 Jun 2008 by grjolly1 and written by Thelma Faye Cain Prince; Ancestry.com: mediaui-viewer/tree;
www.Ancestry.com – multiple sites for "Jolly"
www. en.wikipedia.org/wiki/Battle_of_Stono_Ferry
Carter, Jimmy: *The Hornet's Nest* (New York: Simo & Schuster, 2003)
www.mitchellfarms.com

Kay Byrd

THE MCINNIS FAMILY

How does the McInnis family relate to the Byrd family? Daniel and Sarah Jane McInnis were the parents of John McInnis. John and Nancy McIntyre McInnis were the parents of Effy McInnis who married John C. McLaurin. Their daughter, Sarah Caroline McLaurin, married H. A. David McNeil, and the McNeil's daughter was Effie Leona. Effie married James Edward Byrd, and they were the parents of Edward Leavell Byrd whose son was Hersey Davis Byrd.

The genealogy of the McInnis family begins with **Daniel McInnis** who was a man of mystery. He applied for a pension for his Revolutionary War experience in 1832, but he had difficulty remembering important information. He could not say exactly when he had been born but thought it was "about the year 1754 about March." He said he had lived in Bladen County, North Carolina, ten years after his service in the Revolutionary War had expired, and he said "he was a volunteer and was to stand his draft when called on but was not drafted for a longer time than ten days or two weeks for service." He did not remember the given names of his superior officers either. He had no enlistment or discharge papers. His application for a pension was denied.

Daniel McInnis said he was born in Scotland and obviously had emigrated to America at some point prior to the Revolutionary War, probably arriving in the port of Wilmington like so many other Scottish immigrants. He was accompanied to the New World by his wife Sarah Jane [maiden name unknown] who was also born in Scotland.

Daniel and Sarah Jane had sixteen children, all born in Argyllshire, Scotland. Therefore, it is assumed than Daniel was born in Argyllshire, Scotland, in March 1754. [Note: Most internet researchers list his date of birth as 1740.]

Their sixteen children were:

Murdock McInnis, 1757, married Christian McDaniel about 1779 in Richmond County, North Carolina;
David Norris McInnis, born February 10, 1768; married Rachel Rebecca Mathison (born in 1762 in Edinburgh, Scotland) on November 12, 1780; died 1830 in Jackson County, Mississippi;
Norman McInnis, 1760;

Lucy McInnis, 1762;

Archibald McInnis, 1763;

Richard McInnis, 1765;

Mary McInnis, 1766;

Neil McInnis, 1767;

Angus McInnis, 1769;

Daniel McInnis, Jr., 1770;

Donald McInnis, born March 25, 1773; married Nancy Anne McLeod on February 27, 1801, in Richmond County, North Carolina; died July 12, 1855 in Bexley, Greene County, Mississippi;

Malcolm McInnis, 1775;

James McInnis; 1777;

John McInnis, 1780; married Nancy Y. McIntyre (born December 25, 1790) in Inverness, Scotland. They married about 1811 in Richmond County, North Carolina, and John died on December 10, 1832, in Covington County, Mississippi;

Sarah Jane McInnis, 1781;

Effie McInnis, 1782.

It is not known how many children lived to adulthood or how many children accompanied their parents to America. There is evidence that son Murdock married in Richmond County, North Carolina; that son David Norris McInnis died in Jackson County, Mississippi; and that son Donald McInnis died in Greene County, Mississippi. Apparently, son John and his family moved to Covington County with Daniel and Sarah Jane.

According to his pension application, Daniel testified that he lived in North Carolina for ten years after the Revolutionary War ended on September 3, 1783.

Bladen County began as a vast territory, with indefinite northern and western boundaries. Reductions in its extent began in 1750, when its western part became Anson County. In 1752 the northern part of Bladen County was combined with parts of Granville and Johnston Counties to form Orange County. In 1754 the northern part of what was left of Bladen County became Cumberland County. In 1787 the western part of the now much smaller county became Robeson County. Finally, in 1808 the southern part of Bladen County was combined with part of Brunswick County to form Columbus County. Bladen County is considered the "mother county" of North Carolina because of the 100 counties in North Carolina, 55 of them at one point belonged to Bladen County. It is also the fourth largest county in North Carolina. [Source: en.wikipedia.org/wiki/Bladen County, North Carolina]

Although Daniel indicated that he lived in Bladen County, several of his children married in Richmond County, so the Daniel McInnis family might have actually lived part of those ten years in Richmond County. On the internet there are two land grants awarded to Daniel McInnis in Robeson County. One grant for fifty acres was issued in 1791 and the other fifty acres was issued in 1792. Suffice it to say, Daniel McInnis and family lived in the old Bladen County of North Carolina before moving to the Marion District in South Carolina.

From 1800 to 1814, the Marion District of South Carolina was formed from part of the old Georgetown District, but it was not until 1868-1870 that Marion District became Marion County. Daniel McInnis moved to the Marion District about 1793 and lived there until about 1808 when he moved to Mississippi.

Jackson County, Mississippi, was not formed until 1812, so either Daniel moved to the county before it was designated a county, or he moved after 1812. Covington County was established in 1819, so it is safe to say that Daniel moved north to Covington County after 1819.

The 1830 Federal Census lists one male and one female each aged 80-89 for Daniel McInnis in Covington County. That would make Daniel's date of birth about 1741 and Sarah Jane's birth date about 1750. Slave schedules for Mississippi for the years 1850 and 1860 indicate that they owned two or more slaves.
[Source: Mississippi Slave Schedule, Covington County, 1860, 1850]

There is an old homeplace in Covington County known as the Sarah McInnis place, and there is also a "nearby ford on the river...called Sarah Jane's ford," which refers to Daniel's wife.
[Source: ponder97@bellsouth.net]

Some people say Daniel McInnis was about 90 years old when he died, and his wife lived to be 105. There is an old cemetery in Jefferson Davis County known as the John McInnis Cemetery or the Sarah McInnis Cemetery. It is believed to have been named for Sarah Jane McInnis, Daniel's wife, since she was so old when she died. Neither of their graves has been located.

[Source: ponder97@bellsouth.net]

A description of this cemetery by Ray Easterling of Pascagoula, Mississippi was found on the Internet. He remembers seeing the cemetery when he was a young boy.

> The cemetery was large, and many of the grave markers were cypress and expertly engraved. Some graves [were] visible but not marked at all. I recall a big woods fire and remember several markers were destroyed. I saw some still on fire. My estimate is fifty. Many of the tombstones bore inscriptions relating Scotch and Irish military service, and I was always told [by] an old McInnis descendant that these people were just traveling through.

> The house, known as the Sarah McInnis place, was logs with mud chimney and cypress shingles, as were the stables. I have no idea when they were built, but they rotted away. Some of the largest cedar and crepe myrtle trees I've ever seen were here.
> [Source: An article from a book sent to the author but without title or other documentation, pp. 199-200]

John McInnis:

John McInnis was born about 1780 in Argyllshire, Scotland, and came to the American colonies with his family. He lived his early years in North Carolina and married Nancy Y. McIntyre in Richmond County, North Carolina. Four of their children were born in Richmond County:

Effy McInnis was born on November 20, 1810. [More about Effy later.]

Archibald McInnis was born in 1812 and died on September 16, 1837, in Covington County, Mississippi. He was buried in the John/Sarah McInnis Cemetery in present-day Jefferson Davis County;

Catherine W. McInnis was born on March 15, 1815, married a Mr. Wilkerson, and died on November 14, 1882, in Simpson County. She was buried in the John/Sarah McInnis Cemetery;

Kay Byrd

John McInnis was born on March 28, 1816, married Ann Hubbard in 1836, and died on March 7, 1864, in Covington County. He was also buried in the John/Sarah Cemetery.

[Note: Covington County was established from portions of Wayne and Lawrence Counties on January 5, 1819, less than two years after Mississippi earned statehood. The county was one of the first counties established out of the vast non-agricultural lands in the more eastern part of the state. Simpson County, Mississippi, was formed in 1824 from the Choctaw Cession. The population at the time was 2,329 whites and 829 slaves. Jefferson Davis County was created on March 31, 1906, from Covington and Lawrence Counties.]
[Source: Google Search for Covington, Simpson, and Jefferson Davis Counties, Mississippi]

John and Nancy were pioneer settlers in Mississippi, arriving before statehood. They settled in the Covington County area where they had four more children:

Daniel W. McInnis was born on April 27, 1818, married Nancy Carr in 1847 in Simpson County, and died on June 20, 1899, in Simpson County;

Christian McInnis was born on March 20, 1822, and died on March 20, 1866. She is buried in the John/Sarah McInnis Cemetery;

Sarah Jane McInnis was born on November 17, 1826, and died on March 17, 1867, and is buried in the John/Sarah McInnis Cemetery;

Joseph McInnis was born on February 2, 1828, married Elizabeth Delilah Fairley in 1855, and died on January 28, 1890, in Covington County.

John and Nancy were Presbyterians and were received into the Philadelphus Presbyterian Church in Wayne County on June 28, 1823. [Philadelphus Presbyterian Church is one of the oldest churches in Mississippi, and, according to their website, was "organized by Scottish pioneers who travelled through Georgia and Alabama to Mississippi."]

In time John and Nancy were accepted into membership of Hopewell Presbyterian Church in Jaynesville, Simpson County. Hopewell was organized in 1830 shortly before John's death.

> In 1830 a band of Scotchmen met in an old schoolhouse, located on a farm [owned by the Booth family]...and organized this church. Quiet and unobtrusive, [and] tolerant of all others in their devotions, descendants of the land of the thistle built a community church that has lasted for a century...

> Neill Mathison...erected the church house which has stood during all these years on the banks of Skiff's Creek, a pretty little stream that trickles down through the hills of Jeff Davis County...A gallery was erected in the little church so that the slaves might hear God's Word preached.

> With its hand-hewn heart pine construction and beautifully simple lines, the 157-year-old Hopewell Church is one of the few remaining legacies of the religious dedication of Scottish pioneers who carved out homesteads in the Piney Woods of South Mississippi.
> [Sources: *The Clarion-Ledger*, Jackson, MS, newspaper clippings, 1930, 1987]

In later years, their son John was made an elder, and many McInnis grandchildren were baptized in Hopewell Church.

At the young age of 42 and just three years after the birth of his last child, John McInnis died on December 10, 1832. His cause of death is unknown. He was buried in what became known as the John/Sarah McInnis Cemetery.

In the 1840 and 1850 U. S. Census, his wife Nancy was listed as the head of the household with young children living with her. She and her young children lived near her older childrens' homes, and she probably received assistance from them. After the Civil War, on October 18, 1867, Nancy died and is also buried in the John/Sarah McInnis Cemetery.

There are nineteen land transactions for John McInnis from 1837 to 1859, totaling 1,702.68 acres. Since John the Pioneer died in 1832, it is assumed that his son bought all of this land.

Kay Byrd

Effy McInnis:

The oldest child of John and Nancy McInnis, Effy McInnis was born in Richmond County, North Carolina, on November 20, 1810. She actually grew up in Mississippi where she met the dashing, young John C. McLaurin of the prominent Daniel McLaurin family. They fell in love and were soon married, making their home in Simpson County where they raised six children on their beautifully-sloping, grassy property. They built a new home which is still in existence today. Their children were:

Sarah Caroline McLaurin, born on March 29, 1849, in Simpson County. [More about Sarah Caroline later.]

Nancy Effy McLaurin, born September 7, 1835, in Simpson County, married J. S. Campbelle on December 3, 1873, and died on April 21, 1921. She was buried in the McLaurin Cemetery, Simpson County;

Zebulin Butler McLaurin, born on January 17, 1837, and died on December 7, 1858, while attending the University of Mississippi. He was also buried in the McLaurin Cemetery, Simpson County;

Archibald Hugh "Pearl River Hugh" McLaurin, born on September 6, 1838, married Cora Wilson, and died on March 11, 1906, in Bridgeport, Simpson County. He was buried in the Pleasant Hill Cemetery, Simpson County;

Mary Catherine McLaurin, born in 1840, married Thomas Jefferson Scarborough, and died on January 19, 1881. She was also buried in the McLaurin Cemetery, Simpson County;

Cornelia McLaurin was born on November 20, 1844, married Archie Fairley on February 14, 1877, and died on January 4, 1883, in Lawrence County.

Effy, John, and their children were active members of Hopewell Presbyterian Church. John was an early elder of the church and participated in various church activities and matters of business.

Although the family may not have been wealthy, they were certainly prominent members of the Jaynesville community of Simpson County. They owned slaves and grew a variety of crops, both for their own use and for cash money. They were well-off enough to send their son to the University in Oxford. [More information can be found about this family in the chapter entitled The McLaurin Family.]

Effy died on June 5, 1865, in Simpson County, and John died on April 4, 1887. Both are buried in the McLaurin Cemetery in Simpson County.

Sarah Caroline McLaurin:

The youngest child of Effy and John McLaurin was Sarah Caroline who was born on March 29, 1849. Sarah was only twelve years old when the Civil War began, and like other households in Mississippi, life was dictated by the battles fought in this war. Her older brother, Archibald Hugh (nicknamed "Pearl River Hugh") was in the Mississippi 46th Infantry, Company B. Two brothers-in-law also served in the Confederate Army before they married Sarah's sisters.

After the war Henry Adam David McNeil moved to the Jaynesville area and bought land. When David met Sarah is unknown, but they married on November 30, 1871. Their first child was still born, but their second child was a daughter whom they named Effie Leona, after Sarah's mother. Another stillborn daughter was born, and then they had their last child, Hugh Alexander McNeil. [More information on this family can be found in the McNeil Family chapter.]

Effie Leona McNeil was born on April 6, 1877, in the Janesville community of Simpson County. She received her education at the French Camp School and Lexington Normal College. She was a schoolteacher, and en route to her first job, met James Edward Byrd. They married on May 11, 1898, and were the parents of seven children who lived to adulthood. Their first son was Edward Leavell Byrd, born on January 28, 1912. [More information on this family can be found in the books, *Traveling Companions* and *Oaks of Righteousness*, by this author.]

On his web page, a McInnis researcher says:

> Highland Scots were lured [to America] by the promise of cheap land they could farm year-round augmented by plentiful game. They were driven from their homeland by high rents, meager income, exhausted farms, and later by the "Clearances". [Highland **Clearances:** the forced eviction of inhabitants of the Highlands and western islands of Scotland, beginning in the mid-

to-late 18th century and continuing intermittently into the mid-19th century. The removals cleared the land of people primarily to allow for the introduction of sheep pastoralism.
[https://www.britannica.com/event/Highland-Clearances]

What they found in North Carolina was the "Pine Barrens" – vast, marshy forests of long leaf pine considered by earlier settlers too difficult to farm. But, in time, these newcomers tamed it.
[Source: Macinnes.org/cairn/Stories/JohnMcInnisHistory.pdf]

In time these hardy men and women moved west and settled in the new State of Mississippi. Here they plowed their fields, built their homes, established their churches, and raised their hard-working, dedicated families to become the backbone of this new country. We owe families like the McInnis Family our gratitude and appreciation for the noble legacy they have left for all who followed.

The link between the McInnis Family and the Byrd Family lies with Effy McInnis who married John McLaurin. Their child, Sarah Caroline, married David McNeil, and their child was Effie Leona McNeil. Leona married James Edward Byrd, and their son was Edward Leavell Byrd. Edward's son was Hersey Davis Byrd.

Sources:

Internet:
   en.wikipedia.org/wiki/Bladen County, North Carolina;
   Mississippi Slave Schedule, Covington County, 1860, 1850;
   Ancestry.com: ponder97@bellsouth.net;
   Google Search for Covington, Simpson, and Jefferson Davis
      Counties, Mississippi;
   www.britannica.com/event/Highland-Clearances;
   Macinnes.org/cairn/Stories/JohnMcInnisHistory.pdf.
An article from a book sent to the author but without title or other
   documentation.
The Clarion-Ledger, Jackson, MS, newspaper clippings, 1930, 1987.
Family Papers
On-site Visits

Kin

THE McLAURIN FAMILY

How does the McLaurin Family relate to the Byrd Family? Sarah Caroline McLaurin married H.A.D. McNeil. Their child, Effie Leona McNeil, married James Edward Byrd. Leona and Edward were the parents of Edward Leavell Byrd, who was the father of Hersey Davis Byrd.

The McLaurin Family have kept good records of their family history and have generously shared much of their information with the Byrd Family. Some of the following information was taken from the internet and other sources, but a major portion is directly lifted from information obtained from the McLaurin Family notes.

There are a number of theories as to the origin of this family, but since there were often references to their Scotch-Irish ancestry by the Byrd children, perhaps the best information can be found in the book, *Scottish Clan & Family Encyclopedia (Collins)*:

> The clan Lauren of old composed a part of that celebrated tribe, the Scotti or Dalriada, which came originally from the continent, settled first in Ireland, crossed over into Scotland in the year 503 or thereabouts, where, by bravery and ability, it eventually succeeded in subduing the country and in changing the name of ancient Caldonia into Scotland. The *Encyclopedia Britannica* says: 'The transfer of the name was due to the rise and progress of those Scots called Dalriad, which migrated from Dalriade, Antrim, Ireland, to Argyll in the beginning of the sixth century. Irish traditions represent these Scots as Milesians from Spain.'"

[Source: *Scottish Clan & Family Encyclopedia, page 237*]

The name "Laurin" was derived from the settler's name, Loarn, which seems to be a "modification of the name of Saint Lawrence who suffered martyrdom under Valerian in 251 A. D."
[Source: www.unc.edu/~ecanada/maclarun].

The author of *Scottish Clan & Family Encyclopedia* continues:

> The cast of face, the straight, high nose of this tribe and the names Andrew, Alexander, Cornelius and others would seem to denote a Grecian origin, and this would seem to be borne out of the fact that the Leseii were Greeks who settled in Ionia in Asia

102

Kay Byrd

Minor, from Atticus, Greece, and became very powerful and aggressive people.
[Source: www.unc.edu/!ecanada/mcclan]

In Scotland much of the lands held by the Clan were north of Glasgow on the western side of Scotland around and including the present-day town of Appin in Argyllshire. For much of its early history the MacLaurins were a clan in high favor with the King of Scotland whom they supported in battle, but around the 12th century, the "MacLaurins were reduced from the condition of proprietors to that of 'kyndly' or perpetual tenant." Although the king was reminded that the MacLaurins had done much to improve the land and support the king, the clan nevertheless lost favor with the Crown.

"Among the most distinguished members of this clan (in earlier days) was Collin MacLaurin, son of a clergyman in Argyle. Collin was a professor of mathematics in the Colleges of Aberdeen and Edinburgh and was a friend and companion of Sir Isaac Newton. He translated the psalms into Gaelic and his brilliant writings secured for him the friendship of the most eminent men of the day. His textbooks on mathematics are still used in Scotland and in France. His son, Lord Dreghorne, was an author of repute, and a senator of the College of Justice, Edinburgh..."
[Source: www.unc.edu/~ecanada/mcclan].

The Byrd Family kin begins in 1590 with the birth of (first name unknown) McLaurin and his unknown wife who became the parents of Daniel McLaurin (born in 1610). This Daniel McLaurin was apparently a minister who married a girl from the Stewart clan. Their children were **John** (born about 1645) and possibly Daniel, Jr., (born about 1165). John and his wife (also a Stewart) were the parents of another John (born in 1680 in Argyllshire and sometimes called John "of Culloden;" Hugh (born about 1685 in Argyllshire); **Christian** (born about 1690 in Argyllshire); and Dougal (birth date unknown).

Christian McLaurin was married to a Miss Cameron, and they had at least four sons and possibly one daughter. The children were: Hugh (born January 29, 1720/21 in Glenahyle, Argyllshire); Duncan (born February 12, 1723/24 in Appin, Argyllshire); and **Daniel** (born about 1730 in Appin, Argyllshire); and Christian (whose birth date is unknown). Their daughter was Margaret, who married Alexander Chisholm.

Kin

Daniel McLaurin married a Miss McColl and they lived and died in Scotland, but they did not want their children to remain in that country. During the 18th Century, many MacLaurin families chose to emigrate to America for reasons unlike some of their countrymen. They were not destitute, nor were they gold- diggers. As one writer said, "It was no lack of prosperity nor desire to better their fortunes that led these parents to take this step, for they carried on a large...[farm]...in one of the most fertile and picturesque parts of Scotland. Their home was a large, white house...in the beautiful glen near Loch Etive, surrounded by majestic mountains and situated upon a stream so clear that the salmon could be seen lying twenty-four feet below..." The motivation for moving lay in the laws of conscription during the 1700s. Since the Year 1745, when there was a clan uprising, the law stated that all young men must serve in the army. Many of the families, including the MacLaurins, were weary of war and the deaths of so many young highlanders; therefore, when their sons reached the age of eighteen, "they determined to leave home and country rather than part with any of their children."
[Source: unc.edu...]

"Sixteen families of the name MacLaurin...all more or less related and doubtless leaving Scotland for the same cause, sailed from Appin, Argyllshire, Scotland, in 1790, and did not reach Wilmington, North Carolina [for months] owing to the ship's getting out of her course. Water had become very scarce and it was a wearied lot that finally stepped ashore in the new world." Among these families were the children of Daniel McLaurin and his wife:

Laughlin, born 1760 on the Isle of Skye, Scotland; married Sarah Annie McColl; died 1822 in Mississippi;

Duncan "Major" McLaurin, born between 1760 and 1779 in Appin, Argyllshire, Scotland; married Nancy Carmichael;

Mary, born before 1765 in Appin, Argyllshire, Scotland; married John McKay;

Daniel McLaurin, Jr., born 1766 in Appin; married Nancy Calhoun; and died in 1845 in Simpson County, Mississippi;

Hector McLaurin, born about 1768 in Appin;

Abigail "Effie" McLaurin, born 1769 in Appin; married Alexander Fairly; died in 1831 in Mississippi;
Hugh R. McLaurin, born between 1779 and 1780 in Appin; married Sarah [unknown last name]; died between 1840 and 1850;

Neill McLaurin, born 1771 in Appin; married (Catherine) McMillan in 1802; died in 1827;

John Duncan McLaurin, born between 1760 and 1770 in Appin; married (1) Sallie Cameron; (2) Mary Catherine McIntire; died 1823/24 in Mississippi.

All the sons of Daniel McLaurin were graduates of the University of Edinburgh and placed a high premium on education. They wrote letters back to Scotland, and, as with other Scottish immigrants, they encouraged their friends, neighbors, and clansmen to come to America.

The children settled for a while in Marlboro County, South Carolina. There some of them met and married their spouses and established their first homes. Many of their children were born in Marlboro County, but, like so many other Scottish immigrants, they soon left the Carolinas and moved to Mississippi.

Many of the children's cousins settled in Richmond [now Scotland] County, North Carolina, and eventually established the town of Laurinburg, North Carolina, as the county seat. It was said that the town was "named in honor of the badge of the clan – a sprig of mountain laurel." Other McLaurin descendants moved to Virginia, Florida, and to Nashville, Tennessee, where "Augustine and Effie McLaurin Shepherd made a fortune in the wholesale boot and shoe business..."
[Source: www.unc.edu...]

One of Daniel's sons, Laughlin McLaurin, and his children moved to Rankin County, Mississippi, and after the birth of their son Anselm Joseph, moved to Smith County, where the rest of their seven children were born. A newspaper clipping saved for many years by Effie Leona McNeil Byrd describes the accomplishments of these McLaurin brothers and distant cousins of Effie and her brother Hugh:

...All of the McLaurin brothers were lawyers, save two. They were of Scottish descent, their father being the Hon. Laughlin

McLaurin, who was himself a member of the Mississippi House of Representatives off and on for over 30 years. Each of the eight brothers was a stalwart Democrat and every one of them was of powerful physique.

The elder brother of the "Clan McLaurin" was Anselm Joseph.... He attended the common schools and Somerville Institute. He enlisted in the Confederate Army in 1864 and served as a private. The war over, he again attended the Somerville Institute, 1865-1867. He studied law and was admitted to the Bar in 1868. He began practice at Raleigh. He was elected district attorney in 1871; a member of the House of Representatives in 1879; Democratic presidential elector for the state at large in 1883; delegate to the constitutional convention of 1890; elected as a Democrat to the U. S. Senate to fill the vacancy caused by....Sen. E. C. Walthall...Senator McLaurin served from February 1894 to March 1895. He was elected governor of Mississippi in 1895 and served from 1896 to 1900. He was elected to the U. S. Senate in 1900...and re-elected without opposition in 1907. He served from March 1901 until his death in Brandon on December 22, 1909.

Next to Governor McLaurin in age was Dr. Albert Gallatin McLaurin. Dr. McLaurin was a delegate to the constitutional convention of 1890, which made the organic law under which Mississippians live, the franchise articles on which not only rid the Commonwealth of ignorance and incompetency but became a guide and a model for other Southern states. Dr. McLaurin was elected as a delegate to that historic convention from the County of Smith where he was born and reared.

The third McLaurin brother was Hon. Horace Jehu McLaurin, who for a number of years after leaving Smith County, lived at Rolling Fork in Sharkey County, and represented his senatorial district in the Mississippi senate. Senator McLaurin was a delegate from Sharkey County in the constitutional convention of 1890, being the third member of the McLaurin family to occupy seats in that great body of patriotic Mississippians. The secretary of that convention...in calling the roll of that body, said, "McLaurin of Rankin, McLaurin of Smith, McLaurin of Sharkey." It is doubtful if any other three brothers ever represented any state in the same constitutional convention. Hon. H. J. McLaurin was a lawyer and a planter.

The fourth McLaurin brother was Hon. Robert Sylvester McLaurin, who moved from Smith County to Brandon, Rankin County, where he engaged in the practice of law. He was elected district attorney continuously for some 20 years. The district was a large one comprising a number of counties and for many years Mr. McLaurin held the office without opposition.

The fifth brother of the "McLaurin clan" was Hon. William K. McLaurin who moved from Smith County first to Sharkey and later to Vicksburg, Warren County. He represented the great County of Warren several times in the state Senate of Mississippi and was a circuit judge for a number of years.

The sixth brother was Hon. George Walter McLaurin, who removed from Smith County to Vicksburg in Warren County. He was elected and re-elected a member of the Mississippi Railroad Commission, when each of the three commissioners of that body were members of the Mississippi Board of Prison Control. Walter McLaurin was a lawyer and his acquaintance was co-extensive [sic] with the state. It was said of him that he perhaps knew more people and could call them by their given name than even his distinguished brother, Senator and Governor McLaurin, who used to say that any man who had known him for 24 hours and did not call him "Anse" was not his friend.

The seventh brother was Hon. Wallace McLaurin, who moved from Smith County to Brandon, Rankin County. Wallace McLaurin was appointed receiver of public moneys at Jackson, Mississippi, by Grover Cleveland during his first administration and was later the secretary of his brother, Hon. A. J. McLaurin while he was a U. S. Senator. During the second administration of Cleveland, he was for a time inspector of minerals in several of the territories.

The eighth McLaurin brother is the Hon. Sidney Lee McLaurin, who also moved from Smith County to Brandon, where he yet resides. He has seemed not to have had political aspirations, holding only two minor offices. In his early manhood he was secretary of the Mississippi Railroad Commission and five years ago he consented to accept the office of Supervisor of his Beat and was chosen without opposition. He was made president of that body. It seems that his friends and neighbors thought that he could be of service to his beat and county in the matter of better highway building, and he made the sacrifice holding that office for four years but declining to stand for re-election. As a result of his presidency of the Board of Supervisors of Rankin County, the building of a magnificent highway running from the east bank of Pearl River through Brandon, the county seat of Rankin, connecting the East and West Highway—which runs from Meridian to Vicksburg through Jackson—near Pelahatchie, was started and is now being rapidly constructed. Mr. McLaurin is one of the leading lawyers of the state.

The newspaper concludes its article with a mention of the children of Governor A. J. McLaurin:

A brilliant daughter of Hon. A. J. McLaurin, Mrs. Daisy McLaurin Stevens, who possesses political acumen and the knowledge of statecraft equal to Gertrude Atherton—the great author of *The Conqueror*—was unanimously chosen a member of the National Democratic Committee by the Mississippi State Democratic Convention when it met to select delegates to the National Democratic Convention in New York, that nominated Davis and Bryan—the next president and vice-president of the United States. [Note: In 1924 John W. Davis and Charles W. Bryan were the Democratic candidates for U. S. President and Vice President. Evidently this article appeared in the Jackson, Mississippi, *Clarion Ledger* sometime during 1923 or 1924.]

Mrs. Stevens attended the National Democratic Convention in New York, and the senatorial and other friends of her gifted father, who met this charming woman on that occasion, are reported to have said that she possesses the magnetism and brilliancy of Senator McLaurin. Hon. Forrest Stevens, the lamented and talented husband of Mrs. Stevens, was an able circuit judge for a number of years.

Hon. Anselm Joseph McLaurin, the only son of Senator A. J. McLaurin, born and reared in Brandon, was twice elected circuit judge of his district. He resigned during his second incumbency to become a member of the well-known and able law firm of May,

Sanders & McLaurin of the capital city. Mr. McLaurin is a fine lawyer and his popularity is co-extensive [sic] with the state.

All of the McLaurin brothers, except Sidney, are dead. No family in Mississippi, to such large degree and covering such a period of time, has left its political imprint and official holding on this Commonwealth.

By: Edgar S. Wilson

[Apparently this article was from the Jackson, Mississippi, *Clarion-Ledger*, dated 1923 or 1924.]

In another article on the McLaurins, the newspaper reports the following sad story:

...At 4 o'clock Friday evening a telephone call from Brandon informed the people of Jackson that the governor's daughter, Mary, was dying and a few minutes later there came another message that her pure young spirit had winged his flight.

Death is always sad to someone, but in this particular instance, it was peculiarly so, not only to the immediate family, but to the citizens of the State generally, all of whom are more or less interested. Coming as it did on the very eve of the adjournment of the Legislature, the announcement of the death of the Governor's daughter has enforced the absence of the chief executive, clogged the wheels of legislation, interrupted the business of a great commonwealth, and cast a pall of gloom over an entire state.

Of the sympathy of his people, the Governor may rest assured— it was manifested yesterday in unmistakable terms, when it was known that his daughter had really breathed her last, and at most, within a few moments after her father and mother had reached her bedside, a "silence deep as death" pervaded the atmosphere of the legislative halls, while lawmakers, judges and others in high official places, spoke in whispers and trod as softly through the long corridors as if the cruel monster had just invaded their own homes.

Those who knew the bright, and as they saw her last, rosy-cheeked girl, could not restrain their emotion and did not attempt to hide their tears. Mary was the Governor's fourth daughter—a bonny, bright-hearted lass, whom none knew but to love; a father's joy and a mother's companion, the life of her home, the delight of her schoolmates, and the pride of her teachers.

On Friday, March 27th, [1901] Mary McLaurin would have attained her seventeenth year, and would also have graduated with the first honors of her class at the Brandon Female College next June, after which she was to make her home with her parents at the executive mansion in this city. But as inscrutable Providence had decreed otherwise—that she should become an inmate of that beautiful "mansion in the skies," and thence she was gone...

Governor McLaurin had one other child, Sallie, who was born on April 18, 1877, and died one year later on April 18, 1878, according to Internet information.
[Source: www.worldconnect.rootsweb.com...McLaurin].

Although the entire McLaurin clan/family were characterized by excellent mental capabilities, strong faith in God and active participation in the Presbyterian church, aptitude for public service, strength of character, healthy bodies and longevity, not all the descendants of Daniel McLaurin were as famous and politically active as the sons of Laughlin McLaurin.

Daniel McLaurin, Jr.

The Byrd ancestors were the sons and daughters of Daniel McLaurin, Jr., and his wife Nancy Calhoun [Scottish spelling *Calquhoun* or *Colquhoun*]. Daniel, Jr., was born in 1776 in Appin, Argyllshire, Scotland, and with his siblings arrived in the United States in 1790. He married his first cousin, Nancy Calhoun, in 1799. Nancy was born probably in Scotland and came to this country with her parents, Effie McLaurin and John Calhoun.

[Note on the Clan Colquhoun: Clan Colquhoun is one of the oldest highland families of Scotland and has occupied and controlled an estate of thousands of acres on the west bank of Loch Lomond for over 800 years. This information was taken from the Clan Colquohoun Society of North America on the Internet.]

Daniel McLaurin, Jr.'s name was first found in Richmond County, North Carolina, and later in the records of Marlborough District, South Carolina, where he moved with his wife and established a home. All eight of their children were born in Marlboro County, South Carolina.

Mary was born in 1795. She married Isaac Carr and became the matriarch of a long line of Mississippi Carr descendants. She died in 1841. Her children were:
John Washington Carr, Martha Emmaline Carr, William Calhoun Carr, Catherine Elizabeth Carr, Daniel Frederick Carr, Emanuel Carr, and Hugh Carr. Each of these children likewise had children, thus the long line of descendants;

Daniel, III, was born in 1800 and died in 1821;

Effie Abigail was born in 1806 and, like her older sister, married a Carr. Her husband was Joseph Carr, but it is unknown if the two Carrs were related. Effie died after 1860;

John Calquhoun McLaurin was born on August 31, 1811, married Effie McInnis, and died in Simpson County, Mississippi, on April 4, 1887. [More details on this ancestor will follow];

Hugh Calhoun was born on September 30, 1813, married Harriett Emily Love, and died on July 13, 1880. He became a doctor and was the father of five children: Daniel, Nancy, Hugh, Sally, and another daughter who married Carl Callaway;

Duncan, known as "Speckled" Duncan [origin of the nickname is unknown] was born on October 5, 1815, and married Christian McCollum. Their children were: Daniel L., Catherine, Archibald L., and Nancy Black. Speckled Duncan died on January 31, 1884;

Catherine McLaurin married Lachlan McFarland. She was born in 1816 and died before 1847;

Laughlin (or Laucklin) McLaurin was born in 1817, married Lavinia Barlow, and died in 1862. His quite accomplished children are listed in the above article from the Jackson, Mississippi, newspaper, *Clarion Ledger.*

Kin

The wife of Daniel, Jr., and the mother of the above children, Nancy McLaurin, died in 1821 in Wayne County, Mississippi, which was the same year of the death of her oldest son, Daniel McLaurin, III. Although the cause of their deaths is unknown, it is interesting to speculate that perhaps a disease killed both of them.

After Nancy's death, Daniel moved to Simpson County, Mississippi, and most of his children moved with him. He built a home in the Jaynesville community of Simpson County, which still stands today, and lived there the rest of his life, doing business as a farmer/planter. There was an interesting article on the Internet entitled, "Remembering Seventy-One McLaurin Slaves – 1847." It included the following verse:

> I know why the caged bird sings, ah me,
> When his wing is bruised and his bosom sore,
> When he beats his bars and he would be free;
> It is not a carol of joy or glee,
> But a prayer that he sends from his heart's deep core,
> But a plea, that upward to Heaven he flings –
> I know why the caged bird sings!
> By Paul Laurent Dunbar, Poet

A receipt for the purchase of 71 Negro slaves by Daniel and John D. McLaurin, brothers, in the amount of $37,000 lists some of the slave names:

Harry, aged twenty-three	Lucy, aged fifty-four
Jude, aged fifty-two	Leave, aged forty-nine
Mark, aged twenty-one	Lucy, aged nine
Crease, aged twenty-five	Judy, aged nine
Stephen, aged twenty	Rachel, aged ten
Doctor, aged fourteen	Mandy, aged seven
Washington, aged twelve	Beda, aged five
Isaac, aged twenty-seven	Leah, aged three
Charles, aged twenty-two	Jane, aged one day
Emanuel, aged one	Esther, aged thirty-five
Martin, aged two	Mary, aged eight
Etc., etc.	

The receipt ended with:

Which said negroes I warrant and defend to the said Daniel and John D. McLaurin, their heirs, executors and administrators against the lawful claim or claims of all and every person and persons whatsoever to be sound in body and mind and subject to no bodily infirmity given under my hand and seal this the 11th day of November AD 1847.

(Signed) Duncan McLaurin

The brothers might have bought the slaves for the entire family. The website continues with the following information:

[NOTE: The bill of sale only had seventy names.]

According to the 1850 Simpson County Slave Schedule:
John D. McLaurin had 53 slaves;
John McLaurin had 2 slaves;
Duncan McLaurin had 10 slaves
Hugh McLaurin had 10 slaves.

According to the 1860 Simpson County Slave Schedule:
Duncan A. McLaurin had 20 slaves;
John C. McLaurin had 5 slaves;
Hugh C. McLaurin had 58 slaves;
John D. McLaurin had 76 slaves.

[Source: McLaurin Family Papers, Collection Number Z/510F; www.angelfire.com/folk/gljmr/McLarin.html]

Daniel became a member, perhaps even a charter member, of Hopewell Presbyterian Church near the confluence of the Covington, Simpson, and Jeff Davis County lines. The following brief history of this church appeared in an article in a Mississippi newspaper announcing plans for the church's Sesquicentennial Celebration:

Hopewell Presbyterian Church was organized in April of 1830. The meeting place was an old log school house owned by D. W. McLaurin, located about five miles south of the present building. It consisted of one large room with a pulpit at the head. Hewn logs were used for pews. Since there was no instrument, the song leader had to hum a note to "raise the tune."

Although the church was organized during the pastorate of the Reverend Jacob Richow, the first regular pastor was the Reverend P. H. Fullinwider, who served from 1830 until 1834.

The present building, excluding the Sunday school rooms and the porch, was completed before 1857 by Neil Mathison, who had been awarded the contract. The lumber used was heart pine that was hand planed. The congregation voted April 16, 1950, to add Sunday school rooms and a porch. The church has been kept up over all these years and is still in excellent condition.

An interesting story is told by one of Daniel McLaurin, Jr.'s descendants:

One spring Sunday afternoon about 1960 my Aunt Zilla and Uncle Braxton McNair went with me to the old Daniel McLaurin home in Jaynesville in Simpson County. There we found the family Bible in the possession of Miss Rachel McLaurin, a granddaughter of Daniel McLaurin Jr. Miss Rachel was then eighty years old. My aunt and uncle, being of Presbyterian faith, had known Miss Rachel from church meetings, so while I was busy copying the Bible records, they were carrying on a very interesting conversation. My uncle asked about some young man in the family whom they had known, and Miss Rachel quickly said that he had fallen a long way from his upbringing, that he was a big Baptist preacher now. For the first time in my life, I kept quiet about my Baptist faith!

Her next little tale about Grandpa Daniel revealed much of his strong religious convictions. She told about his visit to a nearby Baptist church service and it happened to be on an occasion when they were observing the Lord's Supper. Of course, his Baptist neighbor failed to pass the wine and bread to their Presbyterian friend. At the end of the services, when everyone started out of the church, Grandpa Daniel made his way toward the front. When asked where he was going, his reply was, "That's the Lord's table down there and I aim to have some of it!"

[Source: unc.edu/~ecanada/danielmc.html]

John Calquhoun McLaurin

John Calquhoun McLaurin was born around 1811 in Marlboro County, South Carolina. With his family he moved to Mississippi around 1816, first to Wayne County and then in 1821 to Simpson County. He married Effy McInnis who was born on November 20, 1810.

Like his father and siblings, John established his home in the Jaynesville community of Simpson County. He was a farmer/planter and, as mentioned above, a slave owner.

He was active in Hopewell Presbyterian Church and was made an elder in the early 1850s. From church minutes, it is evident that John McLaurin was a regular attender and was present on most business meeting occasions. He was once asked to serve on a special committee that investigated the conduct of one Mary Weathersby. On July 24, 1875,

> The session met at the house of J. C. McLaurin according to adjournment. Opened by prayer by present Rev. Joseph Gilbert, moderator...J. C. McLaurin, having been appointed a committee to inquire into the case of the rumor against the Christian character of Miss Mary Weathersby, made the following report...that he has taken some pains in the investigation and that there is sufficient proof to convict Miss Mary Weathersby of fornication and also of profane swearing; but the testimony is from those who probably will appear before the session and cannot be forced to do so.
>
> The following resolution was passed that Miss Mary Weathersby be cited to appear before the session at the church on the fourth Saturday of August 1875 to answer to the following charges: Unchristian conduct...that is such conduct as amounts to fornication to be proven by the following witnesses: L. A. McCaskill, W. W. Dampier, Martin Williamson, Ingram Patterson, Eliza Williamson.
>
> Submitted by A. Wilkinson, Clerk of Session

Apparently, Miss Weathersby chose not to appear at the next session so the "session passed a resolution to issue a second citation." Still Miss Weathersby did not appear, so the church took the following action: "...Miss Mary Weathersby having been cited to trial the second time refused to appear before the session and is hereby excluded from membership."

[Source: "Hopewell Presbyterian Church Minutes," Library of the Church of the Latter-Day Saints, Salt Lake City, Utah]

John and Effie [sometimes spelled Effy] had at least four daughters and two sons. There may have been other babies stillborn or miscarried, but these are the only living children they produced:

1. Nancy McLaurin was born on September 7, 1835, at home in Simpson County. She married J. S. Campbelle and there were no children born to this union. Nancy lived to be eighty-six years old and died on April 21, 1921. She was buried in the McLaurin Cemetery in South Simpson County, Mississippi.

Although there are references both on the Internet and in some of the Byrd family papers to suggest that Nancy was married to J. S. Campbelle, her tombstone says Nancy "McLaurin" which would indicate that she never married.

A distant relative, Mack Gardner, gave us "the lowdown" on Nancy. It seems Nancy did in fact marry J. S. Campbelle, who had come to town with a group of ditch diggers. [A census record located by Nita Byrd Lumpkin says that J. S. Campbelle was a railroad worker, but the two occupations could be the same. He might have been digging ditches for the railroad.]

Nancy and J. S. built a house just down the road from Nancy's parents. One day Nancy went out on the porch and asked her husband what he was doing. He was sharpening his razor, and he said, "I'm going to cut your throat." He was not joking, and Nancy fled the house. She ran down by the river, over to her parents' home and told her father about the threat. John McLaurin pulled out his fox horn [a cow horn which made a deafening sound and used for emergencies] and blew. Neighbors came running. They all went over to Nancy's house, and J. S. Campbelle was never seen again.

The black woman who worked for Nancy later told the McLaurin family that she had seen blood in one of the rooms of Nancy's house, meaning that J. S. Campbelle had probably been killed, but no further action was taken.

Another mystery arises from a story told to Nita Lumpkin by her grandmother, Effie McNeil Byrd. There is some evidence that Effie's aunt lived near the French Academy where Effie and some cousins attended school. Effie and her cousins lived with an "unmarried aunt while attending French Academy." Her aunt had very little money and sometimes there was not enough food to go around. On one such occasion someone in the family group caught a bird, perhaps a blue jay, de-feathered it, gutted it, washed it, cooked it, and ate it for supper!

The house was often cold as well since money for heat was in short supply. Originally it was thought that Nancy McLaurin was this aunt, but if she had married J S. Campbelle, this might be a mistaken assumption. There were two unmarried McInnis sisters and one of them could have been the aunt in question.

2. Zebulon Butler McLaurin was the first son born to John and Effie McLaurin. He was born on January 17, 1837, near Bowie Creek in Simpson County. Like his kinsmen Zebulon was an intelligent fellow and at the appropriate age he enrolled in the University of Mississippi at Oxford, Mississippi. College was not what Zebulon expected, and for a while he could not adjust. He was not interested in studying or even being at college. His father sent him a lengthy letter:

Simpson Co., Mississippi
Oct. 30th, 1858

Zebulon, Dear Son,

I should have written to you soon after you left but when Duncan returned, he said you were not going to stay at Oxford if everything did not suit. Consequently, I waited to know where to write. And some two or three letters have been received in the neighborhood: your mother one, and the doctor one.

You stated in your mother's that you had done very little in the way of studying. I hope you have by this time made all the necessary arrangements and have got fairly under way and will apply yourself with all possible diligence. The way is open for you and it is for you now to make good the opportunity. And you must apply yourself or time and money will affect

117

nothing. You should not let anything else draw your attention nor in any way disturb your studies. You should come up to the expectations of your friends and disappoint those that wish you would fall behind— some that have taken a course in that institution without much gain to themselves or satisfaction to anyone. And although you have come in contact with young giants in intellect and may seem at first to be greatly your superiors, let it not for one moment daunt you, but rather, take courage and contend nobly for the prize.

You are now far away from home and friends, hence the many restraints that seemed to linger round you, you have past their bounds. But recollect there is one eye that sees you; and you should always look to your heavenly father to guide you through this life's rugged steeps, and if you put your trust and implicit confidence in him, he will do thee good all thy days. In your studies, he is a great teacher and a never-failing friend. Look to him, for it is he that giveth and it is he that taketh away, and he giveth liberally to all that asketh.

Indulge me now while we hold a pleasant talk, and I speak the more freely to you knowing that you will hear me and may I not say that I know you will listen to my words. And you know that I want you to do well and to succeed in all your undertakings. And you have the greatest assurance that if you look to him you never will fail, for he says seek first wisdom of me and I will add all things unto you. He will keep you from temptation and he will be a present help in every time of need. If he is for you, who can be against you? But to turn to another theme...

...I want you to keep this letter and refer to it if you should begin to lag or tire by the way and to make you look to God to help you in the way you should go. But to your studies, there is [sic] many things to draw you off and to attract your attention. But you should never allow yourself to be drawn from your studies. That should be the pole star as long as you are there. Surmount all difficulties that may come in the way. Those books you have is [sic] the work of some man; are you not able with the advantage you have to go through and accomplish some great work? There is not a possibility of your failure, if you will try. Now will you not? I know you will.

Zebulon, I have reversed the common rule in this letter. I have left the things that relate to the family for the last. We are all well at this time and have not had any sickness since you left. Hugh [Zebulon's younger brother, age 20 at the time of this letter] has been very sick again, worse than he was the first time. I carried the doctor out to Wilson's on Thursday, and I brought him home on Monday following. He went back this morning; he lost three weeks. The doctor's children has [sic] been sick. Duncan's children has [sic] all been sick. And Hugh is pretty sick, cold. All the rest of our relatives and friends, all well. Nothing new or of great importance has taken place since you left. Doctor Lauchlin has had three or four spells of chill and fever; was some better the last we heard. My crop is not good, neither corn nor cotton. I have not ginned any cotton yet and have gathered but little corn. John E. McNair beat Stine 1950 votes. McMillan beat Sturges 1000. Walker beat Banks 50. May beat Lenn 22 votes. [Note: This was probably a local election.]

Zebulon, I must come to a close. Direct your letters to Hugh, Rockport, Copiah Co., Miss. Write a full account of all things in relation to our class.

I ever remain your affectionate father, /s/J. C. McLaurin

A month later his uncle, Duncan A. McLaurin [the younger brother of Zebulon's father] also wrote him. The main thrust of this letter was the same as that of Zebulon's father. Both men were trying to encourage Zebulon to study hard and do well in school. Duncan reported that Zebulon's brother was well again and going back to his school. He mentioned that the children had been sick and one little Negro died from pneumonia. He ended the letter with "Accept the love of an uncle," and signed it "D. A. McLaurin."

During the course of one winter Zebulon became quite ill and, despite the doctor's best efforts, Zebulon died on December 7, 1858, in his college dorm room. A cousin sent the following letter home to Zebulon's parents:

University of Mississippi
Dec. 8th, 1858

Dear John,

Yesterday, even yesterday, it was not so much a task to write. But this morning what shall I say? Bowed down under heavy afflictions we may lament; we can even endure. But when man dieth and goeth to his long home, where is he? Zebulon is no more. If his departure has caused us to grieve, what must it not bring upon you. May He who has given and who has taken away interpose his merciful hand and lighten your afflictions is the prayer of your nephew.

Daniel B. Carr

P. S. Zebulon died 23 minutes after 8 o'clock Tuesday 7th Dec. p.m. He passed away without a struggle and without manifesting any degree of pain. He got weaker and his breath was shorter and shorter till finally he ceased to breathe. He knew everyone that went into his room till a short time (two or three hours) before his death. But the doctor saw his brain was affected and that he was not in his right mind for two days. He would make an occasional remark Sunday morning that seemed somewhat strange, but we thought his restlessness caused it. The doctor thought he was doing so well Saturday that it was not worthwhile to prescribe anything. His sickness was short and his suffering brief. D.B.C.

3. The next child born to John and Effy McLaurin was also a boy whom they named Archibald Hugh McLaurin. He was born in 1839 at the McLaurin home on Bowie Creek. He married Cora Wilson (1844-1924), and they also made their home in Simpson County. They were the parents of at least three children, and these three are mentioned in several papers of Effie McNeil Byrd. They are cousins De, Turner, and Alethia. Archibald died in 1906. For some reason Hugh became known as "Pearl River

Hugh," but the origin of that nickname is unknown. In a letter dated 1980 to Valois Byrd, Hugh's granddaughter Edna May wrote that she "liked that" nickname.

4. Mary Catherine was born next on November 27, 1840. Like her siblings Catherine was born at home in Simpson County. Mary Catherine married Thomas Jefferson Scarborough from Lawrence County, Mississippi. Catherine and T. J. had two sons and at least three daughters. The boys were John D. and William. Internet sources seem to disagree a bit on the names of the girls, but the best source lists them as Carrie, Mary, and Martha. Some also add Nancy, or Nan, but that is more likely a reference to Catherine's sister, Nancy McLaurin, who lived with them some of the time. A picture of the Scarborough family on Ancestry.com shows two younger girls and one younger son. Catherine died on January 19, 1881, in Simpson County, Mississippi.
[Source:
http://trees.ancestry.com/tree//5625265/person/147154654/media/1?ft m+1]

5. Cornelia McLaurin was born in 1845. On February 14, 1877, Cornelia married Archie Fairly from Lawrence County, Mississippi. The only two children found for this family are Margaret E. and Nannie C. They lived in Lawrence County, and on the 1880 U. S. Census, Richard Campbell lived with them as a laborer. Cornelia's date of death is unknown.

6. **Sarah Caroline McLaurin** was born on March 29, 1849, in Simpson County. In the Hopewell Presbyterian Church minutes, she was identified as the daughter of John C. and Effy McLaurin and her birth date was noted. On June 25, 1895, she was baptized by the Rev. A. R. Graves.

After the Civil War Sarah Caroline married Henry Adam David McNeil, and they established their home in the Jaynesville community of Simpson County. David was a farmer/planter and Sarah Caroline was a homemaker.

Their first little baby girl died at birth on July 11, 1873, as did another little girl born on September 15, 1879. However, on April 6, 1877, Effie Leona was born, quite alive and quite healthy. Then in 1883 David and Caroline became the parents of a son whom they named Hugh Alexander.

From all indications the family was close. Grandchildren fondly remember buggy and horseback rides out to the Jaynesville area to visit their grandparents and remembered the times when their Grandfather McNeil would travel to Mount Olive to worship at the "big" Presbyterian church located there.

David and Sarah Caroline remained active members of Hopewell Presbyterian Church throughout their lives and faithfully brought their children to church with them. The children were taught Christian principles at home, and the children were expected to do their share of the work, both on the farm and in the house.

Like other McLaurins, David and Sarah Caroline insisted that their children be educated and sent them away to preparatory school and to college. They were insistent that their daughter meet her teaching obligations before marriage and had the wedding of their daughter in their home after she had fulfilled her teaching duties.

Sarah Caroline McNeil died of a "stomach ailment" at age 67 on January 6, 1916, although David lived to be 83 years old, dying on March 20, 1924, at the home of their son in Magee, Mississippi. Both Sarah Caroline and David are buried in the Hopewell Presbyterian Church Cemetery.

The old McLaurin home place in Simpson County is still standing and is currently owned by John McLaurin, a descendant of the family of which Sarah Caroline was a part. John lives in Memphis, Tennessee, but several years ago his mother, Evelyn Knight McLaurin, extended a cordial invitation for any of the Byrd family to tour the home by pre-arranging a visit with her son John.

A cousin, Mack Gardner, graciously met with Davis Byrd, Nita Byrd Lumpkin, and Kay Byrd in Mount Olive, Mississippi. He took us to Hopewell Presbyterian Church and provided us with information about the church and allowed us to take photographs of the interior. Then he guided us to the church's cemetery where we took pictures of the gravestones of McLaurin and McNeil ancestors.

Mr. Gardner opened the old McLaurin home and gave us a guided tour of each room as well as explanations of furnishings, pictures, and memorabilia. He provided us with lunch and showed us several letters from McLaurin ancestors.

Then we were escorted to the McLaurin Cemetery, which is located in a gated field belonging to neighbors, and where we discovered the graves of many more McLaurin ancestors. We drove passed Bowie Creek and were shown the approximate location of the home and lands once owned by H.A. David and Sarah Caroline McLaurin McNeil.

Effie Leona McNeil:

Leona was named for her maternal grandmother, Effy McInnis McLaurin. As mentioned above, she was well educated. She attended French Academy, a Presbyterian preparatory school, and graduated from Lexington Normal College. Both schools were located in Lexington, Mississippi.

Prior to her marriage Leona taught school in Bassville, Mississippi. On May 11, 1898, she became the bride of James Edward Byrd of Mount Olive, Mississippi. Effie and Edward were the parents of eight children, seven of whom lived to adulthood. The first child was stillborn.

A full story of Leona and her life can be found in the book, *Traveling Companions,* by this author, under the section entitled "Effie Leona McNeil Byrd."

Suffice it to say that the McLaurin family provided a proud heritage. They were intelligent, religious, and civic-minded and became leaders both in the Country of Scotland and later in the United States.

From Leona McInnis McLaurin and John C. McLaurin, and their daughter Sarah Carolina McLaurin and her husband, H. A. David McNeil, as well as the next generation of Effie Leona McNeil and James Edward Byrd, the link between the McLaurin and the Byrd families is complete. Leona and James Edward Byrd were the parents of Edward Leavell Byrd, who was the father of Hersey Davis Byrd.

Sources:

Scottish Clan & Family Encyclopedia (1994: HarperCollins Publishing);
Internet:
  www.unc.edu/~ecanada/maclaurin;
  www.unc.edu/~ecanada/mcclan;
  www.unc.edu/~ecanada/origin;
  www.unc.edu/~ecanada/danielmc.html;
  www.angelfire.com/folk/gljmr/McLaurin: "Remembering Seventy-One
    McLaurin Slaves – 1847" and Receipt for Purchase of Slaves by
    Daniel and John McLaurin;
  www.worldconnect.rootsweb.com...McLaurin;
  www.ancestry.com search for various family members;
  www.ancestry.com/tree/5625265/person/147154654/media/1?ftm+1;
  Google Search: "Daniel McLaurin, Jr." and Clan Colquhoun Society of
    North America;
Undated Newspaper Clippings from the *Clarion Ledger*, Jackson
  Mississippi;
Genealogy compiled by Edna May McLaurin;
Library of the Church of the Latter-Day Saints: "Hopewell Presbyterian
  Church Minutes," Salt Lake City, Utah;
Personal Papers of the McLaurin and Byrd Families;
McLaurin Family Papers, Collection Number Z/510F;
Personal Visits and Observations.

THE McLENDON FAMILY

How does the McLendon Family relate to the Byrd Family? The mother of Hersey Davis Byrd was Nora Brown Byrd. Nora's mother was Hattie Jane Ball Brown and her grandmother was Margaret Lou Boggan Ball. Margaret's mother was Nancy Jane McLendon.

[Note: There were numerous spellings of the name of McLendon: MackLenna, MackLandin, MackLendon, McClendon, and McLendon. Through the decades the spelling changed several times until it seemed to be universally established as McLendon. "Though MacLandins appears to be a Scottish name, the name Dennis is distinctly Irish."
[Source: dmcclendonblog.wordpress.com/heritage/the-original/]

The first known McLendon in this country was Dennis Macklendon of the Colony of North Carolina. He arrived sometime prior to 1696 along with his wife, Elizabeth and four sons: Francis, Dennis, Bryan, and Thomas. There are at least two theories as to his homeland and parentage. According to Richard R. Dietz on the website "gwest," the "generally accepted story" is that Dennis MacLendon came to North Carolina from Scotland and was the son of John MacLennan.

Other theories as to the homeland of the McLendons say that Dennis MackLendon was the son of Bryan MacLandins of Barbados and his wife, Margery Hunt, daughter of Henry Hunt of Barbados. Bryan MacLandins was a wealthy planter in Barbados, but he probably arrived there as an indentured servant prior to 1660. Upon his father's death, Dennis inherited the plantation in Barbados, but since "economic opportunity was poor on the island, Dennis sold the plantation, left sometime prior to 1687, and sailed to the American colonies."
[Source: www.gwest.org/mclmyth.htm. by Richard R. Dietz]

Some researchers say Dennis settled first in Virginia, probably Nansemond County and later relocated to Perquimans County in North Carolina. These areas are near each other and the dividing line between Virginia and North Carolina was not established for good until 1779.

> The Albemarle Sound settlements were separated from Virginia when Charles II granted the new province of Carolina to the Lords Proprietors. The provinces were divided at the 36th parallel by the Carolina charter of 1663; the Carolina charter of 1665 moved the line northward to

36°30', adding a 30-mile-wide strip to Carolina. By 1680 Virginia authorities were becoming irritated by residents along the boundary region who refused to pay their Virginia quitrents. The Virginians preferred to ignore the provisions of the 1665 Carolina charter and considered that the boundary should be at the 36th parallel, as outlined in 1663, which would place the most heavily populated districts of Carolina in Virginia.

Attempts at surveying a boundary were frustrated by various private interests and objections from Virginia, which feared that a boundary survey would extinguish their claims to the land around the Albemarle settlements. Virginia even ordered a secret survey in 1705 to see how much land would be lost by an accurate survey. When North Carolina became a royal colony as the Lords Proprietors sold their rights to the province, the Crown insisted on a boundary survey. In 1728 commissioners and surveyors from both provinces began work on settling the location of the boundary. The line was begun at Currituck Inlet on 5 March 1728, and 73 miles were surveyed when work halted six weeks later. Work was resumed in the fall. After an additional 50 miles were surveyed, the North Carolina commissioners left for home, declaring that it was a waste of time to survey so far inland and so far from any settlers. The Virginia party continued surveying for another 72 miles, getting as far as present-day Stokes County.

The Virginian point of view of the 1728 survey was set forth by William Byrd II in his famous *History of the Dividing Line betwixt Virginia and North Carolina* (published in 1841). Byrd noted the plight of planters whose lands were divided by the line, "which made the Owners accountable to both Governments." He also wrote that many settlers in the area preferred to belong to North Carolina, where the grasp of the government was weak and taxes for the province and the church were lower. Further surveys in 1749 and 1779 traced the remainder of the boundary. The surveys simply continued the line surveyed in Byrd's time, with little controversy. [Source: https://www.ncpedia.org/boundaries-state]

Wherever he came from, Dennis Macklendon integrated well into the society of his newfound home. He "proved eleven rights for which he received 550 acres of land" citing himself, his wife, and his children. In 1700 he proved thirteen rights, again naming his family and perhaps some slaves, and thus acquiring more land. [Source: Dietz]

He "became allied with the leading families in the Province" and was named a "Justice of the Peace as early as 1705." The court was actually held in his home since he was one of "His Majesties Justices." At other times, he was a member of the jury, "being chosen with eleven other wise and just gentlemen."
[Source:
https://moorecountywallaces.com/histories/McLendons%20of%20Anson %20County.pdf]

Dennis' first wife died sometime prior to 1702. His second wife was a widow, Deborah Astine Sutton Whedbee. Her first marriage was to "Nathaniel Sutton who had died in 1682, leaving her with four children: George, Joseph, Nathaniel and Rebecca Sutton [who was an early ancestor of the Byrd family]. Her second husband was John Whedbee who died in 1697 leaving her with two more children: Richard and Deborah Whedbee." She had no children with Dennis Macklendon.

The children of Dennis Macklenden and his first wife Elizabeth settled in North Carolina and each acquired many acres of land. Son Bryan, possibly named for his Grandfather Bryan MacLandins of Barbados, received a land grant for 130 acres in Carteret County, North Carolina, in 1739.

Son Francis and his wife, also named Frances, bought and sold lands in what was then Bertie Precinct and he received a land grant in 1722 for 418 acres in Perquimans County; another 630 acres in Bertie Precinct in 1727, another 600 acres in Craven County in 1738, and a final 600 acres in Craven County in 1744. These counties were neighboring counties and, when new counties were formed, some of this property probably overlapped.

Son Thomas received eleven land grants in Craven County. "He claimed seventeen in his family, some of whom could have been slaves." Thomas was "prominent as a Road Commissioner and a vestryman in St. Patrick's Parish in New Bern," North Carolina.
[Source: moorecountywallaces.com]

Dennis McClendon, Jr., lived in Anson County, North Carolina, and was well acquainted with early ancestors of the Boggan family, namely James Boggan and his brother Captain Patrick Boggan. Like his father, Dennis was a prominent settler in Anson County, fought in the Revolutionary War, and established a good name for the McLendon family.
[Source: WikiTree: Descendants of Dennis McClendon]

Some of the land transfers for Dennis, Jr. indicate that he was born in Scotland about 1680. He married Margaret Early, the daughter of John and Mary Early, in North Carolina in 1700. Dennis, Jr. died in 1725 and his will is recorded in Bertie County. He mentions children: Sons Dennis McClendon [III] and John and daughters Mary and Elizabeth who also obtained land grants in Bertie Precinct in 1727.
[Source: moorecountywallaces.com]

Dennis McClendon III (1702-1784) married Elizabeth Dunn (1706-after 1786) and, at some point, they moved to Camden County, South Carolina, where they lived until their deaths 1784. At least one son born to this couple was John McClendon.

John McClendon (1732) married Elizabeth Ball (1725-1781). They were married on May 25, 1762, probably in South Carolina. They named their son Dennis McLendon IV.

Dennis McLendon IV married Delilah Beasley. Dennis was born in 1762 in South Carolina and was the father of two children, William Buck McLendon and Elias McLendon. Dennis, Delilah, and their children moved to Mississippi. Some researchers say they first lived in Lawrence County and later moved to Simpson County. Delilah died in Simpson County, and after her death, Dennis married Anna, but her surname is unknown. This Dennis McLendon died in Simpson County in 1863. He and both of his wives are buried in the McLendon Cemetery in Simpson County.

William Isom "Buck" McLendon was born sometime between 1794 and 1800 "near the head of Sparrow Swamp" in Darlington County, South Carolina. [Looking on today's map, the head of the Sparrow Swamp Creek is located in Ashland, South Carolina, which is northwest of Hartsville. There is actually a swamp named Sparrow Swamp, but it is unknown if Buck McLendon's family lived near the swamp or near the headwaters of the creek which empties into and out of the swamp.]

Buck McLendon married Nancy Moore on February 25, 1819, "on the waters of Black Creek, Darlington District [called a district because the citizens of the low country rejected the title of "county"]. They were married by Rev. Williams, minister of the local Baptist church. Nancy was born on May 25, 1801, in her home on Black Creek. She was the daughter of Anthony Moore (1765-1816) and Keziah Powell Moore (1765-1840).

Buck and Nancy had at least four children. If there were more children born into this family, their names are lost to history. The four children were: Sarah A. McLendon (1828-1830) who died at age 2; Minerva M. McLendon (1832-1834) who died between the ages of one and two; **Nancy Jane McLendon** (1837-1919); and Isham McLendon (1825-1864). Both of the baby girls were buried in the McLendon Cemetery in Simpson County, or at least a marker was placed in this cemetery to commemorate the two little girls. Nancy Jane married Alexander B. Boggan. [More information on their lives can be found in the chapter on the Boggan Family.] Son Isham served in the Civil War, and his life is told in the following obituary found at findagrave.com.

Isham McLendon was the son of William Buck McLendon and the former Nancy Moore. He had three sisters, Sarah, Minerva, and Nancy Jane. After the death of his wife, William would take two more wives and would father three more sons, Charles, Aaron, and Jessee.

Isham was married on December 10, 1853, in Westville, Simpson County, Mississippi, to the former Mary Miles, widow of Henry Deavers and mother of two sons and two daughters. Their union would be blessed with two sons, Needham Buck and Scott, and a daughter, Rebecca. When the War Between the States was in its second month, Isham McLendon enlisted in Co. E, 1st Battalion, Infantry.

By the summer of 1864, things were going badly for the South. Sherman's march to the sea placed the Confederate Army's forces commanded by Lt. Gen. John Bell Hood in harm's way by August 1864. Union forces under the command of Generals Sherman and John M. Schofield had surrounded the City of Atlanta, part of their plan being to destroy the railroad access, thereby cutting off delivery of additional fighting men and supplies to the Confederate force.

In the first week of August, Gen. Hood's men were ordered to a woodsy area near Utoy Creek where fierce fighting broke out. The hostilities were intermittent through August 5, with the Union sustaining much heavier losses than the Confederacy. As the sun rose on the morning of August 6, it was obvious that the Union soldiers had regrouped. The worst of the battle commenced. By August 7, the Union Army had sustained a total of 400 dead and injured; the Confederate casualties numbered 225. Among the Confederate dead lay Pvt. Isham McLendon, aged 38 years, who died from a single shot on August 6.

Three days later, on August 9, 1864, trooper Elijah Husband, who came from the same Mississippi neighborhood as Pvt. McLendon, grabbed an opportunity and swiftly penned a letter to his wife back home, not knowing when it could be posted but wanting to be prepared whenever the opportunity arose. In it, he wrote, "Four men killed, four captured, and 22 wounded. Isham McLendon is among the slain. I was with him. He was shot through the head. I caught him as he fell. He never spoke after he was shot."

Although there appears to be no actual record that states unequivocally that Isham McLendon was laid to rest throughout eternity in this hallowed ground, it is known that all the fighting men who died in the Battle of Utoy Creek were interred in the burial ground adjacent to the little country church. Isham McLendon is on an official US Government record as dying in battle on August 6, 1864, in Fulton County, Georgia, near Atlanta. It can only have been in this battle as no other was fought in the immediate area on that date.

A year after the end of the war, all remains of the fallen Union soldiers were disinterred from this burial ground and re-interred in the newly-established Marietta and Atlanta National Cemetery (now known as Marietta National Cemetery) in Marietta, Georgia. The unmarked Confederate graves were left undisturbed. There are 30 graves known to be those of soldiers of the Confederacy who fell at Utoy Creek.

Source: http://www.gacivilwar.org/story/utoy-cemetery: "During the Battle of Utoy Creek, Utoy Church was used as a field hospital for treating wounded Union and Confederate soldiers. Atlanta's first physician, Dr. Joshua Gilbert, treated the wounded there, and those

soldiers who died from their wounds were buried in Utoy Cemetery. Dr. Gilbert (1815-1889) also is buried there..."
[Source: Obituary on findagrave.com #169546403]

By 1837 Buck and Nancy McLendon were living in Simpson County and owned at least twenty acres of land. They produced four bales of cotton for sale and grew other crops as well. Nancy McLendon died in 1839 and is buried in the McLendon Cemetery in Simpson County. Her mother and grandfather, Keziah Powell Moore and John Powell, also have markers in this Cemetery.

[Note: John Powell died in Burke County, North Carolina, in January 1790, and Keziah Powell Moore died in Darlington, South Carolina, in 1840. The markers record these dates.]

After Nancy's death, Buck married Barbara Rebecca Aaron who was born in the old Orangeburg District of South Carolina, the daughter of William and Barbara Aaron. Buck and Barbara were married on September 10, 1839, "on the waters of O-Pala-hatch-A Creek in Rankin County."

> ...a marker was placed four miles east of Pelahatchie to designate the boundary between the Choctaw Cessions of 1820 (Doak's Stand) and 1830 (Dancing Rabbit Creek). With the signing of the treaty at Doak's stand, the Choctaw Indians ceded to the United States 5,500,000 acres of land in the central and western part of the State, thus opening the door for white settlers to move into this part of Mississippi. They came from Georgia, Alabama, Tennessee, and primarily the Carolinas as part of the Great Westward Movement. During the 1850's, settlers from the Carolinas ventured into these lands and established a community at the site of an old Indian village.
> [Note: Apparently O-Pala-hatch-A was changed to Pelahatchie. This information is from http://pelahatchie.org/our-community/history-of-the-town/]

This couple had seven children: Charles McLendon (1840-1849); Elias McLendon (1842-?); Aaron M. McLendon (1844-1851); Needham McLendon (1846-1922); John Taylor McClendon (1849-?); Jesse McLendon (1851-1930); and Caroline (1853-?). Barbara Rebecca Aaron McLendon died in 1855. She was 36 years old although she had had eight, and possibly nine, children during her short lifetime.

Buck married a third time. This marriage was to Rebecca Reno Hogg Chancellor who had been married twice before. Although the records are not clear on this, Rebecca might have had three sons in her previous marriages. Her sons with Stephen Hogg (her first husband) were Billy and John. With her second marriage to Seaborn Ledbetter Chancellor, she had one son Harrison Chancellor. Then in her third marriage to Buck McLendon she had twins: Barbara Elizabeth (1857-1950) and Jefferson Douglas (1857-1898). The next year Margaret Catherine was born (1858-1921), and the following year Harry Johnson was born (1859-1940).
[Source: Information from various family trees on Ancestry.com]

The McLendon property was in what is now the ghost town of Westville but was a vibrant area in the early days of the county. Bee King wrote an article called *This and That,* and in it he described life in the "good old days in Simpson County." He said:

There was plenty of wild game and game laws were unknown. Everybody kept a pack of five or six dogs for fencing as well as for hunting. It was the custom of the country churches to elect some member as a dog minder. The man selected was usually a young, active, fair-minded fellow, who would do his duty without giving offense to anyone by over-beating his dog. The dog minder's job was very easy until protracted meetings began in the summer. Then it sometimes became a very hard job.

A great many years ago, around 1875, at Macedonia church, [Buck's son] Jesse McLendon was elected dog minder by the membership. He was well-qualified for the [job], being young, active and greatly interested in the affairs of the church. That summer it was announced that a protracted meeting would begin the following Saturday, and that Brother Solomon Hitt would do the preaching. It was also announced that, on Sunday, dinner would be served on the grounds. When that Sunday came, a great crowd of people assembled at the church, coming in buggies, ox wagons, horse wagons, and on horseback. The dogs came too, apparently hundreds of them.

When services began, the church was at once crowded with people, except at the rear of the back benches where a large space was left for mothers to sit in chairs and where pallets were spread for sleeping children.

Brother Hitt was long and lank and noted for his long sermons. Brother Jesse, anxious to hear all that was said by the preacher, took a seat near the front and forgot about the dogs, but his attention was soon called to a dog fight going on at the rear among the sleeping children. He dashed out and securing a heavy buggy whip came back and began to belabor the dogs at a great rate. Repeated blows with the whip soon drove them out of the church, but on the outside, the battle was renewed with new [and] many recruits added to both sides. They came by the dozens from all quarters, dogs of all ages, breeds, and colors. The noise was terrific.

To add to the noise and commotion of the dog fights was the neighing and squealing of five or six little stallions, hitched around the outskirts of the church grounds. With all that noise on the outside, Brother Hitt had a hard time holding the attention of this audience. Finally, after almost wearing out his buggy whip, Brother Jesse broke up the dog fights and sent them yelping in all directions.

He then walked into the church and broke into Brother Hitt's discourse by saying, "Brother Hitt, I'll do my best to keep the worship from being disturbed anymore by these damned dogs." Brother Hitt said, "Amen to that Brother McLendon. Amen to that."

There was no further disturbance by the dogs until the closing song was being sung when the pot-licker hounds set up a most mournful howling that could be heard afar.

Buck McLendon had a total of nineteen children and several of the sons fought in the Civil War. The account of Isham McLendon and his death in Georgia was written above, but there were other sons and probably sons-in-law who also served the Confederacy. One ancestry member wrote that son Elias McLendon was a private in the 6th Regiment of the Mississippi Infantry, Company H. He was "badly wounded at Shiloh."

Another son Needham "Buck" C. McLendon was also a private and was "wounded in both arms and both legs at the Battle of Shiloh, Tennessee. He recovered and remained in the service until the end of the war." After the war he married Frances M. "Fannie" Hayes and was the father of five children. Needham died on September 22, 1922, in Simpson County.

Apparently, John Taylor McLendon served in the Confederate army, too. There are several references for "John McLendon" in the list of Confederate soldiers, so it is difficult to know exactly which regiment was his. All entries were for privates.

There is a notation for a Jesse McLendon in the 7th Regiment, Mississippi, Infantry, Company C. He is listed as a private, but it is unclear if this is the son of Buck McLendon.

Buck McLendon died in 1860 and was buried in the McLendon Cemetery near Mendenhall. He was only sixty years old.

[Note: Many researchers use Dennis McLendon from Nashville, Tennessee, as Buck's father. This Dennis married Winifred Green. Both Dennis and Winifred lived and died in Davidson County, Tennessee. None of the census information for William Buck McLendon lists Tennessee as his birthplace and some do list South Carolina.]

Nancy Jane McLendon was the daughter of William "Buck" McLendon. In 1876 Nancy and her husband Alexander Boggan bought her father's homestead in Westville, Simpson County, Mississippi. Their son William Jesse Boggan and his family lived with them on this property, and her grandson Theo described Nancy as "a small, dainty lady and quite pretty."

The linkage between the McLendon family and the Byrd family is quite long. In short, however, beginning with William Buck McLendon, he and his wife, Nancy Moore McLendon, were the parents of Nancy Jane McLendon. Nancy and her husband, Alexander Boggan, were the grandparents of Hattie Jane Ball Brown who was the mother of Nora Beatrice Brown. Nora married Edward Leavell Byrd, and they were the parents of Hersey Davis Byrd.

Information from an internet site says, "...the McLendon family of North Carolina since 1696 have been prominent leaders in the affairs of their states. From 1750-1810 there was a great migration of McLendons from North Carolina to South Carolina, Georgia, Mississippi, Alabama, Louisiana, Texas, and perhaps other states. We find among them ten soldiers of the War of the Revolution in North Carolina, twelve in Georgia, four in South Carolina, and there are probably others, which the writer has no record. The McLendon name also occurs frequently in the Wars of 1812 and the

War between the States. Towns, counties, streets, churches and public monuments bear the name of McLendon in all of the above-named states.

"Among our kinsmen may be found many average citizens as well as illustrious doctors, lawyers, politicians, statesmen, preachers, farmers, senators, college professors, and teachers, all doing their part in the building of America in many localities of the United States."
[Source: moorecountywallaces.com]

Sources:
  The following sites were recorded by Richard R.Dietz on his website:
  www.gwest.org/mclmyth.htm:
    North Carolina State and Colonial Records, Volume I;
    Grimes Abstracts of Wills of North Carolina;
    Hathaways Genealogical Magazine, Volume I;
    North Carolina Land Grant Office;
    Camden County Deed Book, South Carolina;
    Bertie Precinct Deed Book A;
    Craven County Deed Book 4.
Other Internet Sites:

https://moorecountywallaces.com/histories/McLendons%20of%20Anson%20County.pdf.
https://dmcclendonblog.wordpress.com/heritage/the-original/.
www.wikitree.com/genealogy/McClendon-Descendants-154.
www.gwest.org/mclmyth.htm.
www.findagrave.com/memorial.
www.ancestry.com
www.MyHeritage.com
www.FamilySearch.com.
www.gacivilwar.org/story/utoy-cemetery.
www.ncpedia.org/boundaries-state.
http://pelahatchie.org/our-community/history-of-the-town/.

Personal papers of Nora Brown Byrd.
On-site visits to North Carolina, South Carolina, Tennessee, Mississippi.

THE McNEIL FAMILY

How does the McNeil Family relate to the Byrd Family? Effie Leona McNeil married James Edward Byrd and their first son was Edward Leavell Byrd, who was the father of Hersey Davis Byrd.

The McNeil Family history begins with Henry Adam David McNeil. He was the first McNeil in this lineage, because he changed his surname from McNure to McNeil sometime after the Civil War but before his daughter Leona was born in 1877.

Thus, to know the ancestry of the McNeil Family, it is necessary to trace the McNure family. However, there are several problems. First of all, despite the unusual McNure name, the Internet revealed a host McNures. [On a site in Scotland, there were 65 variations of spelling for the name McNure!] Finding the "right" McNure family has been quite difficult.

It is a fact that the McNures (or McNuir, McNewer, McNeyer, MacNure, McNurr, MackNure, McNuere, MackNure, MacNewr, MacNoor, etc., etc., whatever!) came from Scotland, and most researchers seem to think they came from the Central Lowlands region somewhere between the cities of Inveraray (in the Strathclyde area near the headwaters of the Firth of Clyde) and Stirling, which is located at the "wee" end of the Firth of Forth in the Central Lowlands. Possible counties of origin would include Kinross, Argyll, or Stirlingshire.

In searching the clans of Scotland, it seems the McNures might have been a part of the MacNaughton Clan, whose ancestral home was located at Glen Shira near Inveraray. Or, they might have been a part of the Macfarland Clan, which was a "sept" of the Campbell Clan located in the County of Argyll. Or, they might have been a "sept" of the Buchanan Clan located near Loch Lomond.

According to World Book, "The Central Lowlands are crossed by the valleys of the Clyde, Forth, and Tay Rivers. This region has Scotland's best farmland and most of its mineral resources. Wide, fertile fields and low hills with patches of trees cover the entire region." [If "our" McNures came from the County of Argyll or from the Loch Lomond region, they would have lived in some of the lower Grampian Mountains. So, some McNures took the low roads and some McNures took the high roads!!]

In an Internet article entitled, "Migration Patterns of Our Scottish

Ancestors" by Myra Vanderpool Gormley, the following general information is interesting:

"The Lowlands of Scotland...originally were inhabited by people partly of Teutonic origins; while the Highlands (to the west) were the home of a Celtic population that had come from Ireland in the 6th Century..."

> Several Scottish colonies...were established in the New World in the 17th Century. Among these were Nova Scotia (1629), East Jersey (1683), and South Carolina (1684). The latter two served partly as refugees for religious dissidents...East Jersey for Quakers and **South Carolina for Presbyterians** who at the time were liable to prosecution because the Church of Scotland had an Episcopal constitution. [It is not known when the first McNures came to America, nor the purpose of their emigration.]
>
> By the 1760s emigration from the Highland of Scotland increased and the reason often given was the raising of rents in their homeland. It is estimated that about 25,000 came between 1763 and 1775. A few went to Nova Scotia and Prince Edward Island, but the great majority settled in the 13 colonies. At the time of the American Revolution most Scottish colonists, especially the Highlanders, were loyalists. Afterward many of them left the United States to settle in Canada or return to Scotland...
>
> Most Scots settled in the Southern and Middle Atlantic States in the 17th and 18th centuries...The settlements of the Highlanders were the Cape Fear River and its tributaries in North Carolina and in South Carolina and Georgia...By the 1790 census Pennsylvania, Virginia and North Carolina had the highest proportion of Scottish stock among their inhabitants.
>
> The Scots are often credited with being the forerunners of the western migration of America for by 1773 there were Scots in Kentucky and by 1779 they were across the Ohio River. Descendants of the North Carolina Scot settlers were pioneers in Tennessee and Missouri [and Mississippi!] ...
>
> Most of the Scottish settlers who came prior to 1854 came from the region of Glasgow [Inveraray and Stirling are north of

Glasgow], Lanark, Renfrew and Ayr (21.7%) and Argyll (13.9%]
..."

If your immigrant Scot ancestor came to America in the 18th
Century, he probably was Presbyterian [as was "our" McNures];
though a fair number of the Highlanders were Roman Catholics
and some Scottish Episcopal clergy came to America...

Education was widespread in Scotland and you will find most of
your Scot ancestors were literate. As early as the 17th Century
the immigrants were writing letters home telling of their success
and prosperity and describing the beauty and richness of their
settlements. Many successful settlers sent funds back to the old
country to enable family members to follow...**The Scots
tended to immigrate as families rather than individuals**.
[Emphasis is mine.]

One source said that of the immigrants to the United States, the people
from Scotland were the most literate and the most highly paid! Another
source said the Scottish people had a long history of public education and
placed a high value on learning." [Emphasis is mine, since this is
particularly true of the McNeil/Byrd family!]

It is also a Byrd family tradition that some ancestors were Scotch-Irish.
This basically means the people were Scottish but had moved to Scotland
from Ireland prior to immigrating to the United States.

McNure Ancestors in the United States

It is unknown when the first McNure came to America. There are several
stories that abound. A fellow researcher and distant kinsman, Keith
McNure [Keith.McNure@afams.af.mil], lists the following undocumented
"facts" about the first McNures in America:

1. The first McNure to America came over with Lafayette and
fought in the Revolutionary War. (James McNure fits this story.)

2. The first McNure (male) was brought to America by his sister
when he was a baby. She married and left the baby/child with
the Corleys in South Carolina to raise. (This is the story of John
Samuel McNure as told to me by my grandfather.)

3. The first McNure family came to America and the parents had to go back to Europe to take care of some business. The children were left here with one or more families. On the return trip to America the parents died, and the children were raised by this/these families.

4. Ship manifest: 1840 – James McNure (18) arrives in Delaware.

5. Ship Manifest: 1846 – Henry McNure (44) and Anne McNure (46) arrive in New York.

One of the first mentions of a McNure in America is James McNure who fought in the Revolutionary War. Keith McNure says he has "heard that the first McNure to America is buried in a cemetery which is now under Lake Murray [in South Carolina]. We believe this to be the Revolutionary War James McNure."

There are records of several James McNures as well as a William McNure and a Thomas McNure, all of whom are listed at one time or another in South Carolina, but there is no documentation to definitively link any of them to the Byrd family. Keith McNure has made an appealing guess that "all these McNures could be related as follows (and in no way at present to prove any of this): James McNure (Revolutionary War) had sons Thomas, William, and James. Keith McNure promises to let us know if he "ever find[s] out any of these connections."

There **is** documentation, however, that James McNure was the father of Henry Adam David McNure and, therefore, from this point on, we are on solid footing.

James McNure

James McNure was born about 1798 but his place of birth is unknown. Actually, his date of birth is also uncertain. In the 1850 US census he is recorded as being 47 years old. This would have made his date of birth in 1803. In the 1870 census he is 72 years which would have made his date of birth 1798. The only certain fact is that his name was James McNure and he was the father of Henry Adam David McNure.

James McNure married Christian [or Christina] Eargle who was born about 1808 and the daughter of Michael Eargle, Jr., and Anna Barbara

Wessinger.

Again, Christian's birthdate is questionable. In 1850 she was recorded as being 29 years old, meaning she was born in 1811. In 1870 she is 62 years old, with a date of birth as 1808. Christian was the mother of H.A.D. McNure and that is a recorded fact.

Since James married a girl of German descent in South Carolina, it is assumed that James was living in the United States when they married.

James and Christian lived in the old Lexington District of South Carolina. There is mention made of the family in 1845, and they are listed in the 1840 and 1850 US Federal Census in the County of Lexington, State of South Carolina.

There were five children born to James and Christian McNure:

Martha E. McNure was born in 1839 in Lexington District, South Carolina. She married Henry Anderson Smith [b. 1834 in South Carolina] and they had at least one son, David Monroe Smith [born February 9, 1862], and died on October 26, 1921, in Hines County, Mississippi].

> David married Lenni Florence Hughes, daughter of Stephen Nicholas Hughes and Diana Wiggington, in 1888 in Smith County, Mississippi. She was born on January 2, 1869, and died on April 11, 1938. They had one son: Waldo Emerson Smith, born on January 28, 1894, and died on December 4, 1945, in Memphis, Tennessee.

Henry Adam David McNure was born on November 27, 1841, in Columbia, South Carolina, which was in the old Lexington District [More information about him follows.]

Mary McNure was born in 1843 in the old Lexington District of South Carolina. That is all the information available on Mary at this point.

George W. McNure was born in 1845 and died April 4, 1909. Like David McNure, George fought in the Civil War, and more is written about him later.

Louisa "Lou" Lucinda McNure was born on February 9, 1849, in Lexington District, South Carolina. Lou married John E. Barnett on September 22,

1869, in Mississippi; and they had six children, five of whom lived to adulthood:

Lou Emma Barnett Bennett born 14 Jul 1872; married Bennett; died 28 Feb 1947;

Minnie Barnett, born about 1873, no further information on Minnie;

James E. "Ed" Barnett, born 20 Oct 1880; married Claudie Mae Hardy (1891-1955); had one son Dan Leon Barnett (1918-1940); died 14 Aug 1985 at age 84; buried in Brownsville, Hinds County, Mississippi;

Laura A. Barnett, born 22 Jan 1886; married Cleveland Purvis (1848-1956), had two children (Nannie -1907-1994) and Nola (1918-1999), and died 26 Sept 1969 (aged 83) in Louisiana;

Florence Bertha Barnett, born 2 Apr 1888; married "unknown" Powell; had two sons (Steve L. Powell 1906-1970 who married Elizabeth Green in 1931) and A. B. Powell of West Monroe, Louisiana; had two daughters: Annie Lou Baker of West Monroe, Louisiana, and Margie Powell Goughf of Jackson Mississippi; died 2 Jun 1968 at age 80. She is buried in West Monroe, Quachita Parish Louisiana;

Ethel Leona Barnett, born 15 Jan 1894; married Heber Jackson Conrad; had three children: Marvin Calvin (1915-1980), Helen Elizabeth Conrad Chambless (1918-2011), and Lizzie Mae Conrad Noland (1923-2008); and died 27 Aug 1983 at age 89 in Vicksburg, Warren County, Mississippi.

James and Christian and their children moved to Mississippi at some point prior to the Civil War. They probably settled in Smith County since they are listed in the 1866 Mississippi census in that county.

Henry Adam David McNeil

Kin

Apparently the two brothers, George and David, were in Mississippi prior to the Civil War and residents of Scott or Smith County. Both of them enlisted in the 8th Mississippi Infantry, Company C, the "True Confederates." A handwritten "war record" in our possession states that H. A. D. McNure/McNeil "joined the army in August 1861 at Raleigh, Mississippi."

The 8th Mississippi assembled in Enterprise, Alabama, in August 1861 and mustered into the Confederate forces in October of that year. They served in a number of locations. [NOTE: As I have read the account of the 8th Regiment, Mississippi Infantry, I have been struck with all the marching they did...from Mississippi to Alabama and then marching to Florida...back to northern Alabama...to middle Tennessee...to Chattanooga...to Atlanta...back to Tennessee...to North Carolina...and finally home...to Mississippi...ALL ON FOOT!! No troop carriers, no buses, no trucks, no light aircraft!! At least David McNure was a teamster and got to ride in a wagon but imagine the comfort of a buckboard on the poor roads and fields of this time!]

David McNure served under the able leadership of Lieutenant Colonel Adin McNeill in General Braxton Bragg's brigade from August 18, 1862, until the Battle of Chattanooga in 1863. Although David remained a private throughout the war, his brother George was promoted to sergeant at some point.

The 8th Mississippi fought in the Battle of Stones River [or the Battle of Murfreesboro] and sometime between December 30, 1862, and January 3, 1863, David McNure was "wounded severely in [the] bowels." In January and February 1863, H. A. D. McNure was "in hospital;" and "on detached service" from March through August 1863. Apparently, he was "furloughed from the...hospitals at Atlanta, GA, on March 2, 1863, for a period of thirty days," and, as a result, was docked "one month's pay...for absence without leave." It is unknown where he spent these thirty days.

After Murfreesboro, the 8th Mississippi marched toward Chattanooga and while fighting in this area and gallantly leading the right wing of the Confederate regiment on the Chattanooga Road in November 1863, Lieutenant Colonel Adin McNeill was killed. It was a particularly sad day for David McNure who had greatly admired his leader.

A poem found in some of the Byrd papers sums up the "True Confederates" [author unknown]:

142

Once farmers, now soldier boys of Company C,
Infantry Volunteers...the Eighth Miss'ippi;
One hundred two strong, each vowed with the rest,
To die for their rights, stand firm to the test.

But this War's no fun, and it wasn't a lark,
For boyhood friends would lie dead in the dark;
Stones River to Chickamauga, and one by one,
Young men of the Eighth, young lives came undone.

Came Missionary Ridge, then Lookout Mountain,
And blood of Southern boys flowed as a fountain.
In late '63 winter quarters were made,
The boys needed rest; their courage was paid...

Then on to Resaca and Kennesaw Mountain,
More blood was shed, poured red from the fountain.
Just east of Atlanta, fought hard man-to-man...
(With one thought aplenty: I think I can!)

March again north to the hills of Tennessee,
Tramped the proud remnant...the Eighth Miss'ippi...
Into Spring Hill, through a blizzard of snow,
They'd fought with a fury, but victory wouldn't show;
The next day came Franklin...Oh, God! What a sight,
Sixty commanders lost, and all in one fight!

But the South's dream was sealed, and such a terrible loss,
Two hundred sixty thousand Southern men had paid the final
cost.
Came one last duty, the one they'd long remember,
The day of their parole, the day of their surrender;
Four years' devotion, with sufferings a-plenty,
Of one hundred and two...now less than four and twenty.

[References to a particular family of twin soldiers were omitted.]

There were many losses in the 8th Mississippi and eventually they were
assigned to the army of General Joseph E. Johnston in North Carolina.
They surrendered on April 26, 1865, at Greensboro, North Carolina, and
later "stacked arms" at High Point, North Carolina. David McNure was

present at both the surrender and the stacking of arms and parole. An affidavit to this effect was submitted by Reuben McNair, "who was in the company with Mr. H. A. D. McNeal." The affidavit was signed on December 21, 1932, in Mount Olive, Mississippi.

And so, the war was over for George and David McNure, and they returned to their homes in Mississippi. David was 25 years old and George was only 21.

In 1866 their father bought land in Smith County, and on the 1870 census their father James was recorded as 72 years old. He was a farmer with a personal estate valued at $100. Their mother Christian was 62 years old; and living with them was Reubin B. McNure, who was four years old and had been born in Mississippi. It is assumed that Reubin was a grandchild although his parents are unknown.

Christian McNure received a land grant of 79.95 acres in Smith County in 1879 [signed by President Rutherford P. Hayes] and on the original document, it says "widow of James McNure, deceased." [Interestingly, the original document was handwritten, and it spelled her name "Christian."] Therefore, sometime before 1879 James McNure died, but it is unknown where he was buried. It is assumed, he was buried near their home in Smith County, Mississippi.

The 1900 Census lists George in Hinds County, Mississippi, at the age of 56. He had been married for 28 years to his wife, Mary McNure [no maiden name given]. Mary was born in March 1857 in South Carolina, and they were married in 1872. Mary could read, write, and speak English according to the census information.

George moved to the Confederate Veterans Home at Beauvoir, the former home of Jefferson Davis, in Biloxi, Mississippi, at some point but probably after the death of his wife. He died there on April 12, 1909, and was buried in their cemetery.

Although David might have returned to his parents' home in Smith County, the next documented information is the 1870 US census which shows him living with the Allen Johnson family in Covington County. He is 27 years old and has $500 worth of real estate and a personal worth of $300. Perhaps the Johnson family was living with him! In addition to Allen Johnson, his wife Martha Johnson, sons T. S. and C. G., and daughter M. L. are listed in the household as well as Samary and Vonboor Nightgay.

In 1875, 160 acres were granted to David McNure [signed by Ulysses S. Grant, President] and recorded in the Jackson, Mississippi, land office. It is described as Homestead Certificate #414.

With a name like "McNure" David must have been the brunt of many jokes and name-calling during his early years and certainly in the army. He decided after the Civil War that he would change his name.

He greatly admired his commanding officer, Lt. Col. Adin McNeill, who was killed in the Battle of Chickamauga. McNeill's four brothers (Erastus, Wiley, William, and Malcolm) all died as CSA soldiers from "disease." (Erastus and Wiley enlisted in Company F – "Clark County Rangers," – 8th Regiment, Mississippi Infantry; and William served in Company D, 37th Regiment, Mississippi Infantry as a Second Corporal). Their younger brother Alonzo was born in 1854 but died at the age of six in 1860. Perhaps, David chose to take their surname because all of the sons in that family died, and there was no one left to carry on the McNeill family name.

The epitaph on Adin's grave says:

Dear brother, too hard it seemed that just at the close of the struggle
In which thou hast striven so bravely and the victory won from the foe,
Flying balls thy life which promised so well should take
But thus it was.
And as the sun in silence hid his face
And the enemy in confusion fled,
And the den of battle lulled into stillness
Three shots thy body pierced.
And ended the life of one of whom we were proud
And sent thy spirit to realms of glory.

Before he officially changed his name, however, David paid a visit to the McNeill home. Wiley McNeill, father of the family had died just after the Civil War in 1867, and their little daughter Cordelia Asaline, who was just seven months old, died shortly thereafter.

The poor mother was still living but must have been heart broken. She was a good Christian woman and gave her blessings to David for his honorable tribute to her family. Subsequently, David legally changed his name to McNeil. [Information from Nita Byrd Lumpkin and Mattie C. McNeil, granddaughter of David McNeil]

On November 30, 1871, David married the daughter of John Colquhoun McLaurin and Effy McInnis McLaurin. Her name was Sarah Caroline McLaurin and she was born on March 29, 1849, in Simpson County, which was adjacent to Covington County where David had purchased land.

Caroline and her parents were quite active in the local Hopewell Presbyterian Church where her father served as an elder. Caroline had been baptized at age ten and "applied for admission to [church] membership and was received on examination on May 23, 1869." Her mother died on June 5, 1865, when Caroline was only sixteen years old but she had a sister, Nancy, and two brothers: Archibald Hugh McLaurin [later known as "Pearl River Hugh"] and Zebulon [who died at age 27 while a student at the University of Mississippi in Oxford, Mississippi].
[Source: Hopewell Presbyterian Church minutes, Family Library, Church of the Latter-Day Saints, Salt Lake City, Utah, and family records and pictures.]

David and Caroline [who apparently pronounced her name "Carolyn"] built their home in the Jaynesville [sometimes spelled Janesville] community of Simpson County. He farmed the land and she took care of the home. On July 11, 1873, their first child—a daughter—was still born, and they buried her in the McLaurin Cemetery "located in a pasture in South Simpson County" on Bowie Creek.
[Source: home.earthlink.net/~rooo22/mcclaurin].

On April 6, 1877, a second daughter was born, and they named her Effie Leona McNeil after Caroline's mother. Leona grew up to be a loving, caring daughter who was quite intelligent. She taught school in Bassville Mississippi, after graduating from college and prior to her marriage to James Edward Byrd of Mount Olive, Mississippi, and later became the mother of Melissa Corinne, Juanita Caroline, Annie Ward, Mary Hasseltine, Edward Leavell, Hugh McNeil and Valois Leona Byrd.

Another daughter was born on September 15, 1879, who was also still born. Like her older sister, she was buried in the McLaurin Cemetery in South Simpson County.

On the 1880 US Census David's mother, Christian McNure, was living with David and Caroline. She had purchased about 80 acres of land in Smith County just the year before. It is unknown what happened to the land when she moved in with the McNeils. The date of her death is unknown, so how long she lived with David and Caroline is also unknown.

Finally, on March 19, 1883, a son was born to the McNeils. They named him Hugh Alexander McNeil, probably after Caroline's brother. From all indications he was a good son and, like his older sister, was active in the Hopewell Presbyterian Church. He died in an unfortunate incident on September 11, 1932, and was buried in the Hopewell Presbyterian Church cemetery near his parents.

David and Caroline remained active in church work. In 1881 David was made an elder in the Hopewell Church and, like his father-in-law before him, served faithfully until his death.

The children grew up, married, and lived relatively close to David and Caroline. Leona's children remember his visits to Mount Olive and his attending the "big" Presbyterian church there. He drove a horse and buggy and would often allow his grandchildren, their cousins, and friends to take a ride. He was a gentle, caring man, and Valois Byrd and her cousin Von Nelle Black fondly remember him as having a good sense of humor and being attentive to his grandchildren. From his pictures he appears to be a rather tall, thin man and wore a mustache and beard. Caroline was short, but also thin. She wore her hair parted down the middle and pulled back to a bun at the base of her neck as was the fashion of the day.

On January 6, 1916, Sarah Caroline died after a brief illness. The following newspaper accounts tell of her life and death:

Mrs. McNeil
[from the Mt. Olive paper]

Mrs. McNeil, the venerable mother of Mrs. J. E. Byrd [Effie] of our town, closed her eyes in peaceful death Thursday night of last week, after a brief illness of what attending physicians claim to be stomach trouble.

This good Christian woman was near 60 years of age, and her bountiful life was spent in serving her Master, attending to her family and blessing her friends; and most assuredly her presence will be missed and her place hard to fill in the community. She was a devout Presbyterian and had lived a pure consecrated life, and death had no fear for her. She's gone to receive a well-earned reward promised by her Father to those accepting His rich promises.

She leaves a faithful husband, a devout son and daughter to grieve after her. Her remains were interred in the cemetery at Hopewell church, Friday morning where they will repose in refreshing slumber until the last and final day when God shall declare that "time shall be no more."

Condolence is extended those bowed down by grief, and may He who holds the mysteries of the Universe in His hand, speak words of love to the heart-broken, is the wish of friends.

The burial obsequies were conducted by her faithful pastor, Rev. McDowell, of this place, assisted by Revs. Orrick and McIntosh, all of who [sic] paid beautiful tribute to the life of the deceased.

MRS. SARAH CAROLINE McNEIL

The subject of this notice was born March 27, 1849. She united with the Presbyterian church about the age of seventeen; was united in marriage with Mr. H. A. D. McNeil, November 30, 1871; and died at her home in Covington County, Miss., January 6, 1916.
[Note the county lines were drawn back and forth in the early days. Today her home would have been in Simpson County.]

Mr. John C. McLaurin, the father of Mrs. McNeil, was an efficient and faithful ruling elder of Hopewell church for many years. He was an orthodox Presbyterian of Scotch descent and reared his children in the nurture and admonition of the Lord.

Mrs. McNeil was devoted to the welfare of her church; loved its ordinances and attended faithfully upon all its services. She was the mother of two children, a daughter and a son, whom she trained with scrupulous care. They are both consistent and zealous members of the church. The son is a deacon of Hopewell Presbyterian Church. [The "wayward" daughter had become a Baptist!] Her influence in her home, in the community and the church was always on the side of a pure, Christian morality. She adorned all the walks of life.

A faithful and devoted wife and mother, a consecrated church member has gone to her heavenly reward. The bereaved husband, children and relatives are graciously commended to the tender mercies of our covenant God.

Her funeral was conducted on the afternoon of the seventh, at Hopewell Church, by Rev. Hervy McDowell, and was attended by a large congregation of loving and sympathizing relatives and friends.   W. B. Bingham

David lived eight years after his wife's death and at some point moved into the home of his son Hugh and family. On March 20, 1924, Henry Adam David McNure/McNeil died at the age of 83. Following are newspaper accounts of his death:

H. A. DAVID McNEIL

God has seen fit to take to "that Home not made with hands," one of His elect, Elder H. A. David McNeil. He was born in Columbia, S. C., November 27, 1841, and died at the home of his son, Hugh A. McNeil, of Magee, Miss., March 20, 1924, being eighty-two years, three months and twenty-three days old. He had been a sufferer for over two years, and oftentimes told his pastor that all was well. We feel that we can all but hear the Master say, "Well done, thou good and faithful servant."

His early life was spent in South Carolina, but he later moved to Mississippi. On November 30, 1871, he and Miss Sarah Caroline McLaurin were happily married and the happy union was blessed with two children: Mrs. J. E. Byrd [Effie] of Mt. Olive, Miss., and Mr. H. A. McNeil of Magee, Miss. His wife died some years ago.

He was buried by his wife in the cemetery at Hopewell church.

DEATH OF H. A. McNEIL
[from the Mt. Olive newspaper]

Mr. H. A. McNeil died at the home of his son, Mr. Hugh McNeil, in Magee Wednesday night. He will be buried Friday at Hopewell cemetery. He is the father of Mrs. J. E. Byrd of our town.

Kin

Words of sympathy are extended to his loved ones in this sad hour. He was a Confederate Veteran and had a large host of friends who regret to know of his sad death.

He was a prosperous farmer, a good citizen, a loving father, a devoted husband, a faithful elder. He joined the Hopewell Presbyterian Church sixty years ago, and the greater part of the time has been clerk of the session.

He leaves his son and daughter and a number of grandchildren and many friends to mourn their loss. We weep but not as those who have no hope, for we know in whom he put his trust. We would say then, "Blessed are the dead which died in the Lord from henceforth; yea, saith the Sprit, that they may rest from their labors; and their works do follow them."

Now the laborer's task is o'er;
Now the battle-day is past.
Now upon the farther shore
Lands the voyager at last.
Father, in Thy gracious keeping
Leave we now Thy servant sleeping."

W. A. Hall, Pastor of Hopewell
Church, Collins, Miss.

David was buried in the Hopewell Presbyterian Cemetery beside his wife.

Hugh Alexander McNeil

The only son of David and Caroline McNeil was born on March 19, 1883, and they named him after his mother's brother, Hugh McLaurin. It is unknown where the parents got the name Alexander; maybe they just liked the name.

Hugh and his sister were very good friends and attended rural schools near their home in the Jaynesville community near Mt. Olive. When they were older, they went to live with a "maiden aunt" [possibly Sarah McInnis] "who *kept house* for them and several first cousins, who, thus, grew to have the mutual fondness of brothers and sisters." [Source: Notes from Juanita Byrd Huang] Hugh Byrd writes, "He attended school at Westville and in Henderson, Tennessee."

Hugh married Nannie Ella Calhoun [born on March 19, 1887, in Covington County, Mississippi, and died on September 16, 1974] on November 27, 1907, and to this union were born the following:

> John Kenneth McNeil, born October 12, 1908;
> Martha Caroline [Mattie C.] McNeil, born April 27, 1912;
> Nannie Lou McNeil, born January 28, 1916;
> Twin Sons: Edwin Calhoun McNeil and Edward Byrd McNeil,
> born January 30, 1921.

Nephew Hugh Byrd writes that his Uncle Hugh "was employed in the mercantile business and maintained his farming interest." The family lived in Magee, Mississippi.

The next information about Hugh concerns his death. Hugh had tenant farmers living on his property. One tenant in particular owed him some money, so one evening Hugh went out to the tenant's house to collect. The tenant came out of the house and, from the porch, shot Hugh in the abdomen. According to the newspaper article, "...the shooting climaxed an argument between McNeil and [Alfred] Sullivan, sharecropper on his place, over a crop settlement. Word reaching here said that Sullivan claimed he acted in self-defense." [Magee, Mississippi, was the byline. The name of the newspaper is unknown.] The incident occurred on Friday evening, but Hugh lived until Sunday morning, September 11, 1932. He was 49 years old.

Hugh's funeral service was held at "the Baptist church Sunday afternoon with interment in Hopewell [Presbyterian Church] cemetery. The Rev. W. M. Williams, chaplain at [the] Sanatorium, officiated assisted by the Revs. W. L. Ferrell and the Rev. Mr. Storey." Hugh left behind his wife Nannie, his three sons, and two daughters.

1. John Kenneth McNeil

Kenneth was born on October 12, 1908, in Covington County, Mississippi. He married Corinne Polk, who was born in Jeff Davis County, Mississippi. They had two daughters. Nancy Carolyn McNeil married Gordon Cornell and they had one son, Kenneth Cornell. The other daughter was Donna McNeil, who married Dannie Moore, and they were the parents of Kevin Moore and Malissa Moore. They lived in Buhl, Idaho, at the time of his father's death, but retired to Ft. Worth, Texas. Kenneth was an electrician by profession.

2. Martha Caroline [Mattie C.] McNeil

Martha Caroline [Mattie C] McNeil was born on April 27, 1912, in Covington County, Mississippi. "She attended school in Magee and received her R. N. degree from Methodist Hospital School of Nursing, Memphis Tennessee. She returned to Mississippi to practice her profession."
[Source: Information from Hugh Byrd]

Mattie C married Hugh George Robinson who was born in Mississippi on August 28, 1910. "Hugh George attended Mississippi College in Clinton, Mississippi, and was engaged in farming and the livestock business in Magee and Simpson County, Mississippi. He died on September 1, 1982." Mattie C and Hugh George were the parents of two sons:

> Hugh George Robinson, Jr. [May 7, 1942 – March 28, 1991] who married May Hubbard. He was employed as an auto technician in Magee. Their children are Martha Caroline Robinson; Christy Jo Robinson [who married Chad Winninham and is the mother of Jessica Erin Winninham]; and Jean Marie Robinson.

> The other son of Mattie C and Hugh George was Edward Thomas Robinson. He lived from April 26, 1945, until June 22, 1960, when he died in an accident. A newspaper clipping has the following account of his death:

> **FALL FROM TRUCK CLAIMS LIFE OF MAGEE YOUTH**
> **Last Rites Friday**
> **June 30, 1960**

> Edward Thomas Robinson, 15-year-old son of Mr. & Mrs. Hugh George Robinson, was killed instantly late Wednesday afternoon on Highway 28 when he fell from the back of a pickup truck.

> The shocking announcement of the tragedy was made to his parents while they were enjoying a cook-out with friends and relatives in the back yard at the Robinson residence.

The fact that Edward Thomas possessed an unusual affection for both young and old and the fact that he was affectionately loved by friends of all ages, was emphasized by the bank of floral offerings in his memory which filled three parlors of the Mims Mitchell Funeral Home.

He was truly a missionary of good will and with his big smile and pleasing manner he could be seen carrying packages and groceries home for individuals who were not fortunate enough to own transportation; he would periodically gather beautiful flowers from his own flower garden and deliver them to shut-ins and other friends to place a silver lining on their day; he could be seen tending children here and there just because he loved children; he could be found dividing his time in many ways in bestowing happiness upon others.

Last rites were conducted from the Magee Presbyterian Church, of which he was an active member, at 10 a.m. Friday with Rev. W. B. Hooker officiating, assisted by Rev. Virgil Bryant. Interment followed in the Magee cemetery under the direction of the Mims Mitchell Funeral Homes.

Active pallbearers were Marvin White, Duncan Watkins, W. H. McCallum, Wilton Lang, E. C. Handenson, and Shirley Steel.

Survivors include his parents, Mr. and Mrs. Hugh George Robinson; one brother, George Robinson, maternal grandmother, Mrs. Nannie McNeil; paternal grandmother, Mrs. Julia Robinson, all of Magee.
[Source: Newspaper clipping from an unknown Mississippi newspaper; Information from Hugh Byrd]

3. Nannie Lou McNeil

Nannie Lou McNeil was born on January 28, 1916, and she married Magee Harvison, a Baptist minister in Louisiana. They had five children: Joan Marie Harvison [a resident of Dallas, Texas], Joel Harvison [who lives in Bogalusa, Louisiana] Jerry Harvison [who lives in Baton Rouge], Eddie

Harvison [who also lives in Baton Rouge], and Carol Harvison [who lives in Massachusetts].
[NOTE: The location of Nannie Lou's children is taken from Hugh Byrd from several years ago.]

According to Hugh Byrd, Nannie graduated from high school and worked "for a short time as a beautician. She continued her education and graduated from LSU. Nannie Lou taught school in Louisiana until she retired," then moved to Baton Rouge.
[Source: Information from Hugh Byrd]

4. Edwin Calhoun McNeil

Edwin Calhoun McNeil was born a twin on January 30, 1921, in Magee, Mississippi, and died during World War II. The Byrd family received the following telegram on June 25, 1943, at 11:55 a.m.:

"EDWIN MCNEIL KILLED PLANE CRASH SOUTH CAROLINA BODY BEING RETURNED TO MAGEE" (from Mims Mitchell Funeral Home)

The local Mississippi newspaper article had the following account:

Sgt. Edwin McNeil Dies in Plane Crash

War has again claimed its toll in bloodshed and heartache in Jefferson Davis County. Sgt. Edwin Calhoun McNeil, aerial engineer in the U. S. Army Air Corps, son of Mrs. Nannie McNeil of Prentiss, Route 2, met tragic death in a plane crash at Kingstree, South Carolina, on Wednesday of last week. Sgt. McNeil was stationed at Greenville, S. C., and was on a practice flight when the plane crashed.

Sgt. McNeil was 22 years of age and was a graduate of the Prentiss High School. After finishing school, he assisted with the farming operations on his mother's farm in the Granby community. Soon after Pearl Harbor, he and his twin brother Edward McNeil, went to Mobile where they were engaged in defense work until their induction in September 1942.

The body, accompanied by Sgt. Marsh of New York, a close friend and buddy who had been with him since his induction, arrived at Hattiesburg by train Saturday evening and was carried overland to the home of his brother-in-law and sister, Mr. and Mrs. Hugh George Robinson of Magee, where it lay in state until the last rites, conducted from historic old Hopewell Presbyterian Church, near the Jeff Davis-Simpson county line at 4:00 p.m. Sunday. His pastor, Rev. L. A. Beckman, Jr., officiated, and interment was made in the Hopewell Cemetery.

Members of the Prentiss Post of the American Legion served as active pall bearers, and a firing squad from the Jackson Air Base fired the salute as the body was being lowered into the grave. The flag that draped the casket was removed, tenderly folded, and was presented to his mother by Mr. W. F. Mahaffey of Prentiss, who spoke appropriate words in the brief presentation ceremony. A mixed octette [sic] from Prentiss furnished appropriate music, with Mary Kathryn Parker as accompanist.

Besides his mother, Mrs. Nannie E. McNeil and his twin brother, Cpl. Edward McNeil of Fort Knox, Ky, immediate survivors are another brother, Kenneth McNeil of Houston, Texas, and two sisters, Mrs. Hugh George Robinson of Magee and Mrs. Magee Harvison of Mobile.

5. Edward Byrd McNeil

Edwin's twin brother, Edward Byrd McNeil, was born in Magee, Mississippi, on January 30, 1921. He lived most of his life in Prentiss, Mississippi, where he graduated from Prentiss High School. Like his brother Edwin, Edward worked in Mobile in defense work prior to joining the army during World War II. He served with the U. S. Army's Armored Division under General George S. Patton. He fought at the Battle of the Bulge and received the Bronze Star.

Edward was a 32nd degree Scottish Rite mason and a member of Bissell Baptist Church in Tupelo, Mississippi. He worked for South Central Bell Telephone Company until his retirement.

Edward married Mary Houston and they had two children: Hugh Edward McNeil who married Germaine Gilgo and was the father of Brian, Jason, and Alison McNeil; and Cherle Jean McNeil who married a Mr. Moore and had one son named Casey.

Edward was a friendly fellow and, according to his obituary, "enjoyed spending time with his Hardee's coffee drinkers."

Edward died on Tuesday, December 20, 2005. His wife Mary lived until July 17, 2015. Both are buried in the Tupelo Memorial Park Cemetery in Tupelo, Lee County, Mississippi.

Effie Leona McNeil Byrd

Leona was the eldest child and only living daughter of David and Caroline McNeil. She was born on the farm near the site of the town of Mt. Olive, Mississippi. With her brother Hugh she studied in rural schools near her home and then lived with a maiden aunt and studied at Old Westfield. Later she was graduated from French Camp Academy, a Presbyterian school, and Lexington Normal College.
[Source: Biography written by her daughter Juanita Byrd Huang in 1962]

When her father accompanied her to her first teaching position in Bassfield, Mississippi, they spent the night in the home of John King Byrd, an acquaintance of her father's who lived in the Rock Hill community on the other side of Mt. Olive. There she was introduced to James Edward Byrd, the eldest son of the Byrd family. He was immediately smitten with Miss McNeil and corresponded with her during her first year of teaching. He would often surprise her and visit with her in Bassfield.

Later Leona became the bride of James Edward Byrd, and they made their first home in Rock Hill where they owned and operated a community general store. Edward was elected to the State Legislature, and while he was away tending to state business, Leona ran the store. Soon the young couple moved to the new town of Mt. Olive, Mississippi.

Leona had been brought up in a Presbyterian home, and her husband was a Baptist. When the first child was old enough to go to Sunday school, Leona was baptized in the Baptist church.

Leona and Edward had eight children. The first child was a son and he was stillborn. Then came Melissa Corinne, Juanita Caroline, Annie Ward, and Mary Hasseltine followed by Edward Leavell, Hugh McNeil, and Leona Valois.

After the children were born, Leona centered all her activities on home, church, and school. She was a charter member of Mississippi P. T. A. She was faithful to Sunday school and to the Woman's Missionary Union at the Baptist church. For most of the years of her husband's life, he was State Sunday School Secretary for the Mississippi Baptist Convention; and because of Edward's travel in his work, Leona had chief responsibility for the day-to-day lives of her seven children. In addition, she frequently served as hostess for guests that her husband invited to their home.

Education was important to Leona and Edward. They had lively discussions at home, and each child was expected to learn and perform well in school. All seven children graduated from Mt. Olive High School and from colleges with bachelor's degrees. Most of the children also had master's degrees and even a couple of them held honorary doctorate degrees.

Church was equally important in the Byrd home, and the entire family supported and attended the First Baptist Church of Mt. Olive. Valois Byrd said as teenagers the young people enjoyed revivals at the Baptist, Methodist, and Presbyterian churches, one revival after the other! Daughter Juanita became a Baptist missionary to China; Daughter Annie Ward worked as an editor for the Baptist Sunday School Board and was the first woman executive at this publishing house; and the elder son, Edward, became a Baptist minister.

Leona also enjoyed the company of Byrd relatives, neighbors, and friends in Mt. Olive. She was a member of the Mount Olive Music Lovers Club and probably enjoyed other civic activities as well.

In 1937 her husband died an untimely death due to the elixir of sulfanilamide, which had been prescribed to him for possible flu or a bad cold. The drug was sold untested and over one hundred people in the United States died after consuming the liquid medicine.

A few years after Edward's death, Leona moved to Nashville Tennessee, to make her home with daughter Annie Ward. Soon her youngest daughter, Valois, joined them in the home and taught in the Nashville Public Schools. In Nashville Leona lived happily with mutual friends of the three and engaged in church activities as long as she was able to do so.

All the children lavished loving care on Leona to the end. For some years she was confined to the home because of a frail body but remained alert and interested in all that involved her children, grandchildren, or friends.

After suffering a mild stroke, she was taken to Park View Hospital in Nashville, where she died on December 13, 1962, after suffering another stroke.

A prayer service was held in Nashville and a funeral was held in Mt. Olive. Reverend A. S. Johnston, an intimate friend of the family, officiated. He told the mourners that "many stories of noble women recorded in the Bible are of women raised because of the same qualities Mrs. Byrd exemplified in her life: The excellent wife and mother described in Proverbs; the woman who maintained a room for the hospitality of a prophet; Hannah, who dedicated her child to the Lord; Martha, who busied herself with the domestic duties; and Mary, who loved to sit at the feet of the Master. The comparisons were substantiated by relating specific deeds of a woman he had known well because of his long and intimate association with her husband, J. E. Byrd, and as a frequent guest in their home. He cited such lives as evidence pointing toward immortality."
[Source: Information from Juanita Byrd Huang]

Effie Leona McNeil Byrd was a strong woman. She was a dutiful daughter and daughter-in-law and an exemplary wife. She was a gracious hostess and friend to many. She lived a long, full life and is affectionately remembered by her descendants.

She was the link between the McNeil and Byrd families.

Kay Byrd

Sources:

Google Searches: McNure; Scottish Emigrants to the U.S.;
World Book Online: "The Central Lowlands of Scotland;"
Internet Article: "Migration Patterns of Our Scottish Ancestors" by
Myra Vanderpool Gormley (Copyright 2000 Myra Vanderpool
Gormley) Reprinted from *American Genealogy Magazine*, Vol. 4, No.
1;
Emails from Keith.McNure@afams.af.mil;
Web.archive.org/web/20100529064017/http://mississippicv.org:80/
MS Units/8th_MS_INF.htm;
Byrd Family Papers and Information from Hugh M. Byrd, Nita Byrd
Lumpkin, Juanita Byrd Huang;
Various Mississippi Newspaper Clippings among the Byrd Family
Papers;
Personal On-site Visits.

THE ROGERS FAMILY

How does the Rogers Family relate to the Byrd Family? Mary
Malissa Rogers married John King Byrd, and they were the parents of
James Edward Byrd. J. E. Byrd was the father of Edward Leavell Byrd and
the grandfather of Hersey Davis Byrd.

The Rogers family has a rich history dating back to England where there
is some evidence that ancestors were of noble, and even, royal birth.
Prominent among the Rogers ancestors in England is John Rogers, the
first Protestant martyr in England. "John Rogers was an English
clergyman, Bible translator and commentator. He guided the development
of the Matthew Bible in vernacular English during the reign of Henry VIII
and was the first English Protestant martyr under Queen Mary I of
England, who was determined to restore Roman Catholicism." Children
and grandchildren of the Martyr were afraid to claim him as a family
member, and thus his direct lineage has been difficult to uncover,
however.
[Source:
https://en.wikipedia.org/wiki/John_Rogers_(Bible_editor_and_martyr)

Another significant name in the Rogers genealogy was Thomas Rogers
(1571-January 11, 1621) who "was a Leiden Separatist [from Leiden, The
Netherlands] who traveled in 1620 with his eldest son Joseph...on the
historic voyage of the Pilgrim ship *Mayflower*. [Thomas] was a signatory
to the Mayflower *Compact*, but perished in the winter of 1620-21. His son
Joseph...was too young, at age 17, to sign the *Mayflower Compact*, but
survived to live a long life." Apparently, this Rogers family did not have
direct ties to the Mississippi Rogers, however.
Source:
https://en.wikipedia.org/wiki/Thomas_Rogers_(Mayflower_passenger)

Tracing the lineage of the Covington County Rogers is fraught with
uncertainty. Many amateur genealogists list Timothy Lot Rogers as an
early ancestor. This Timothy was married to Zilpha Parker and they lived
in the old Nansemond County of Virginia. Looking at the map, it seems
that this area was very near the North Carolina border. Gates and Chowan
Counties in North Carolina are very near the Virginia line, and some
genealogists list those counties as the birth place of some people in the
Rogers family. In 1727 William Byrd of Westover in Virginia was asked to
scout the area between Virginia and North Carolina and to establish the
state line between the two states. This was accomplished in 1727-28,

about the time that Timothy Rogers would have lived in Nansemond County, Virginia. It is thus difficult to know just where exactly the Rogers ancestors were born, lived, and died.

One Rogers family researcher posted the following information about Timothy Rogers and an apparent son, Shadrach Rogers:

> I come through Lot [Rogers], Shadrach's brother, born 1755, in Nansemond, Virginia. Shadrach was married in Nansemond in the home of Timothy Rogers, his father. The marriage was performed by a Rev. Riddick, after whom Shadrach named one of his boys. We think he married Hope Bethea. His brother, Lot, married Anna Bethea, sister of Buck Swamp John Bethea.
> In another post, he said, "This Shadrack was named all three Biblical names..."
> [Source:bumsteadsr@hotmail.com]

In his book, *Shadrach & Hopey Rogers and Families*, William Morgan Brown states that "Lot Rogers came from Gates County, North Carolina. However, there was no documentation to tie Lot with Shadrach."

The Shadrack Rogers Daughters of the American Revolution [DAR] chapter in Covington County, Mississippi, refers to the research conducted by Brown in the above-mentioned book. The history of this DAR was written on May 17, 2012, and posted on the Internet:

> Our chapter is named for Shadrach Rogers, who arrived in Mississippi before 1820, according to the 1820 U. S. Federal Census of Lawrence County, Mississippi. On that census, Shadrach was counted in the age category of above 45, and he had been in the same category for the censuses of 1800 and 1820, meaning that he had been born at least by 1755.

> Shadrach's grandson, Timothy Rogers, was included in *Goodspeed's Biographical and Historical Memoirs of Mississippi, Vol. 11*, published in 1891. In his biography, Timothy said that his grandfather, Shadrach, was 'a native of North Carolina, and a soldier in the war of the Revolution who was noted for his bravery and courage, and high sense of honor.'

> Shadrach was married to Hope (Hopey), maiden name unknown. Some have said she was a Bethea, others a Manning,

and some a Reddick. No information has been located that clearly identifies her family. Having a wife named Hope (Hopey), however, has helped to clearly distinguish our Shadrach Rogers from at least one other man of the same name.

According to the 1790, 1800, and 1810 censuses, Shadrach and his family lived in South Carolina before moving to Mississippi. In 1790, Shadrach was in Prince Georges County, Georgetown District, South Carolina. In 1800 and 1820, he had moved further inland to Claremont County, Sumter District, South Carolina.

In Sumter District, **there was another Shadrach Rogers** [emphasis added by author]; this one married to Celia Jordan. Although there were two Shadrachs in the same county, by looking at land records, they can be separated. The other Shadrach lived in northwestern Sumter District. Our Shadrach with wife Hope lived in an area south of Sumter City near the present-day Sumter-Clarendon County line. This was an area near the Old Bethel Baptist Church, and the creek in the area was named Nasty Branch.

Our Shadrach sold a piece of land in South Carolina in October 1818. This is the last recorded deed of his in South Carolina, so he and his family must have moved to Mississippi between October 1818 and June 1820 when the census was taken. Covington County was formed in 1819, but boundary lines between Covington and Lawrence Counties were not clearly defined until 1822. In 1823, Shadrach, Reddick, and Meshack were all on the tax rolls of Covington County. Shadrach remained on the rolls of Covington County until 1827, and then in 1828 Hopey is listed on the tax rolls. This makes it likely that Shadrach died between the dates of the tax rolls in 1827 and 1828.

Finding two Shadrachs in the same county in South Carolina is probably what led to confusion and mixture of the two men's lives. Our Shadrach moved to Mississippi while the other Shadrach stayed in South Carolina and raised his family there. Unfortunately, when original DAR research was done, the service of the Shadrach who remained in South Carolina was claimed by our Shadrach who came to Mississippi. The Shadrach Rogers line is now closed to DAR applicants.

Even though the DAR states that the maiden name of Hope (Hopey) is unknown, most amateur genealogists list her as Hope Bethea, and some also include Manning in her name—Hope (Hopey) Manning Bethea. If the researcher at bumsteadsr@hotmail.com is correct, our Hopey Rogers was born in northeastern South Carolina into the family of Buck Swamp John Bethea. This information seems plausible, but it has not been documented due to courthouse fires and information being destroyed during the Civil War. Still another researcher, Jerry Rodgers, wrote this information about Shadrach on the Internet:

> ...the Timothy Rogers family...are said to be from Nansemond County, VA. He had at least two sons, Shadrach (born 1753) and Lott. The family moved to NC around Gates County, then to South Carolina. Shadrach married Hopey Bethea in SC and Lott married a sister, Anna...

With reliance on the DAR information, we know that Shadrach Rogers was from North Carolina, and if Hope was in fact Hope Manning Bethea, she was from a prominent Bethea family in northeastern South Carolina. The recorded land transfers in this area show that Shadrach and Hope lived in the very same area of South Carolina that was populated with various branches of the Bethea family, which lends credence to Hope being a Bethea.

However, William Morgan Brown has this to say about Hopey:

> There has been speculation that Hopey was a Bethea, a Manning, or a Reddick family member. I have worked extensively with researchers from all of these families, and proof of Hopey belonging to any of these families cannot be proven. She was not mentioned in any of their family histories printed to this point in time.

As stated in the DAR article, census records for 1790 show that Shadrach and Hopey Rogers lived in the Prince George's parish of the old Georgetown District of South Carolina. Located nearby was Lot Rogers, Robert Rogers, Eli and Elisha Rogers, Jesse Rogers, and three John Rogers. Later censuses showed they lived in the old Sumter District, South Carolina. Their first land purchase was 150 acres on Maple Bay on the Little Pee Dee River according to "Georgetown Grants, Volume 11, page 636."

[Source: Anne Eiland at Aeiland0218@yahoo.com]

In addition to the initial purchase, Shadrach and Hopey had a number of land transactions:

- January 6, 1788: Georgetown, Grants Vol. 23, p. 237 – 668 acres, Maple Bay, Little Pee Dee; [400 acres of this land was sold on 26 February 1801 and Hopey was listed on the sale papers.]
- January 28, 1789: Georgetown, Grants Vol. 25, p. 414 – 100 acres, Big Reedy Creek;
- June 8, 1789: Georgetown, Grants Vol. 26, p. 29 - 200 acres, Maple Bay, Little Pee Dee;
- May 7, 1792: Georgetown, Grants Vol. 65, p. 29 – 451 acres, Maple Bay, Little Pee Dee; [This land was sold on 2 November 1808]
- April 16, 1798: Liberty County, Book G, p. 104-7 – 200 acres, Big Grassey Bay.

Then Shadrach began buying land in the Sumter District of South Carolina:

- September 16, 1799: Claremont County, SC, Conveyance Book CC, p. 139-41 - 300 acres, Maple Bay, Black River;
- February 26, 1801: Claremont County, SC, Book B, p 147 – 400 acres, Maple Bay, Little Pee Dee;
- September 11, 1801: Claremont County, SC, Vol. A, p. 204-5 – 100 acres sold; "Hope the wife of the within named Shadrach Rogers did this day appear before me..."
- May 2, 1802: Georgetown, Grants Vol. 66, pp. 250 – 451 acres, Maple Bay, Little Pee Dee; sold remaining plantation acres.
- September 2, 1803: Clarendon County, SC, Book 1, p. 32 – 33 acres, Black River; purchased
- 19 October 1804: Sumter District, SC (Conveyance Book B, pages 395-6) purchased 300 acres;
- 6 February 1807: Sumter District, SC (Conveyance Book BB, page 332) bought 300 acres;
- November 2, 1808: Marion, Book F, p. 67-7 – 401 acres, Maple Bay, Little Pee Dee; sold
- September 23, 1813: Sumter District, SC, Conveyance Book D, p. 263-4 – 150 acres, Nasty Branch;
- 18 December 1813: Sumter District, SC (Conveyance Book D, page 261), sold 146 acres;

- October 5, 1818: Sumter District, SC (Conveyance Book EE, p. 11-2), sold 800 acres, Black River, Nasty Branch in Claremont County (included a release by his wife, Hopey Rogers).
[Source: William Morgan Brown's book, *Rogers-Rodgers: Westward from the Carolinas*]

Shadrach and Hopey Rogers were the parents of eight children, all of whom were born in South Carolina.

Timothy Rogers was born in 1782, married Elizabeth Taylor, and died on November 8, 1846, in East Feliciana Parish, Louisiana. Elizabeth Taylor Rogers was living with her son Whitten Bethea Rogers in the 1850 census. She was 62 years old at that time and had been born in South Carolina.

Riddick [or Reddick] was born on April 9, 1787, in South Carolina, and died on August 18, 1859, in Jasper County, Mississippi. [Note from W. M. Brown: "Reddick is the only son who has his name documented within SC land records as the son of Shadrach and Hopey Rogers." Another note says, "Fortunately, these dates and the birth location were recorded in the Reddick Family Bible."] Reddick married 1) Mary, who died on September 11, 1839, and 2) Elizabeth Cooley.

Ailsey was born on May 12, 1785, in South Carolina, married William Nelson West (born July 31, 1775, in Virginia and died on October 24, 1846, in Tallahatchie County, Mississippi) and died on September 7, 1863, in Smith County, Mississippi.

Nisa was born in 1787 in South Carolina and died in 1849 in Simpson County, Mississippi. She married Esquire B. Thames in 1808 who was born in 1786 in South Carolina and died in Simpson County, Mississippi.

Israel was born on April 2, 1789, in Sumter District, South Carolina. He married Mary Knighton on January 2, 1812 (who was born February 15, 1793, and died on May 9, 1832) and upon her death, Israel married Mrs. Mourning Gardner Sumeral. Israel "fought in the Battle of New Orleans under Captain Timothy Rogers, his brother. He received 160 acres of land for fighting in the War of 1812. This land was in Kansas, and he sold it." [W.M. Brown] Israel died on July 23, 1877, in East Feliciana

Parish, Louisiana, and is buried in the Cumberland Presbyterian Church Cemetery in East Feliciana Parish.

Shadrack, Jr., was born in 1791 and died in 1851. He married Margaret Knighton on July 4, 1811, in Amite County, Mississippi.

Elizabeth was born in 1793 in South Carolina and died in Covington County, Mississippi. She married Matthew Thames in 1819 at Williamsburg, Covington County, Mississippi.

Meshack was born on October 15, 1795, and was married three times:
    1) Elizabeth Lucy Brunson (born on August 17, 1800, in Sumter District, South Carolina, and died in December 1838 in Collins, Covington County, Mississippi), They married on June 30, 1817.
    2) Mary Lucretia Geiger (born on May 20, 1816, in Collins, Covington County, Mississippi, and died in December 1854 in Collins.) They were married in 1839 in Covington County, Mississippi.
    3) Caroline Campbell Purvis, who was born on January 30, 1810, in Pendleton, Anderson District, South Carolina. Meshack had children by his first two wives, and died in Covington County, Mississippi, in December 1869.
[Information from: William Morgan Brown's book, *Rogers-Rodgers: Westward from the Carolinas*]

By the year 1818 Shadrach Rogers had sold all his land holdings in South Carolina and moved his family to Mississippi. "Land in South Carolina was being worn out, and like so many others of that period, the Rogers family decided to head west for...the newly-formed State of Mississippi [where] land was cheap.
[Source: Anne Eiland at aeiland@yahoo.com]

They traveled in caravans with their possessions strapped onto pack horses and hogshead conveyances. (Also traveling with the Rogers' family was Matthew Thames, who later married Elizabeth Rogers, after their arrival in Mississippi)." [Information from a winning essay "written by Mildred Miller, a tenth grade Collins High School student" and quoted in a book by Gwen Keys Hitt entitled, *Covington Crossroads* .]

"They selected a site along a spring-fed creek in what was then Lawrence

County, but became Covington County when the boundaries were redrawn in 1819. It was in this virgin pine forest the family settled, establishing a dynasty of Rogers...that managed to survive the hardships of the Civil War, including the loss of numerous fathers and sons. Rogers Creek bears their name, a tribute to their continued presence in the area." [*Covington Crossroads* and Anne Eiland]

As previously noted, Shadrach apparently died in 1827. "The last record of [Hopey] was the record of her transfer from the Bethel Baptist Church to the Leaf River Baptist Church in Covington County in 1834. Both Shadrach and Hopey are buried in the Meshack Rogers Cemetery near Salem outside Collins, Mississippi. There is a tombstone for Hopey, and the local DAR erected a memorial marker dedicated to Shadrach Rogers.

Meshack Rogers, [Sr.]

According to his family Bible, Meshack Rogers was born on October 15, 1795, the youngest child of Shadrach and Hopey Rogers. [Even though the name is spelled Meshach in the Bible, apparently the family spelled their son's name with a "k," or perhaps it was changed with general usage.]

Meshack met and married his first wife, Elizabeth Lucy Brunson, in South Carolina where they made their home in the old Sumter District. They were married on June 3, 1817, and their first child, Sarah, was born in 1818.

By 1820 "Meshack is recorded on the 1820 Federal Census, living in Lawrence County, Mississippi. His age was given as 25 and Elizabeth was about 20. The tax rolls of Covington County of 1823 show that the family, including his father Shadrach with two slaves and brother Reddick Rogers, had settled near Williamsburg, Covington County, along the banks of Rogers Creek. At that time Speedtown, south of present-day Collins, was the county seat." [Anne Eiland]

In the ensuing years, nine children were born into this family:

Elizabeth was born October 25, 1820;
Nancy Caroline was born August 12, 1823, and died in 1891;
Shadrack Meshack Abednego [III] was born on June 8, 1825
   and died in 1891;
Josiah was born on January 19, 1827, and died in 1864;
Timothy Luther was born on October 30, 1828, and died in 1902;

Marion Norvell was born in October 1830 and died in 1907;

Martha was born on May 27, 1833;

George Benjamin was born on August 14, 1835, and died in 1862;

William M. was born on August 16, 1837, and died in 1929.

The Rogers family first grew corn, potatoes, peas, oats, rice and some cotton. They later began to grow sugar cane, which was ground in wooden mills and cooked in pots and kettles. All of the crops were usually gathered and hauled from the field on ground slides. The cotton was gathered by the men through the day and the lint picked from the seed at night. The men also tanned cowhides from which they made shoes for the family. There were no stores in this early settlement from which to buy clothes and household goods, so everything had to be made by the people themselves." [Information from *Covington Crossroads*]

The 1828 through 1832 Tax Rolls for Covington County show Meshack Rogers and his mother Hopey Rogers [who was fined no poll tax because of her age and who owned two slaves] as Covington County landowners. The 1830 census listed Hopey Rogers, Meshack Rogers, Reddick Rogers, and William S. Rogers.

In the early days of Covington County, settlers erected "brush arbor structures to serve as churches. A framing was made of rough lumber and small logs, then brush (or leafy branches) was piled on top, providing relief from the hot sun. Seats were made from larger split logs." [Anne Eiland] Meshack and his family would have worshipped in one or more of these early structures.

In 1834 Meshack, his wife Elizabeth, and his mother Hopey asked for membership in the Leaf River Baptist Church. From the McCain Library and Archives of the University of Southern Mississippi, Manuscript Collection: Leaf River Baptist Church Minutes, the following information can be found:

> Settlers of the Baptist faith in the upper Leaf River area of Covington County, Mississippi, under the leadership of Elder Norvel Robertson, Sr., pastor of Providence Church, had held monthly meetings in a school house as early as 1820-21. As attendance grew, the meeting was granted permission to receive and baptize and to celebrate the Lord's Supper under the name "The Leaf River Branch of Providence Church." By

1828 settlement in the surrounding area had increased, and the church desired to establish itself as an independent body. With approval of Providence Church, "The Baptist Church of Christ at Leaf River" was constituted as an independent church on September 18, 1829. Between 1829 and 1969 the church had 36 pastors, the first two of whom were the father and son Norvel Robertson Sr. and Norvel Robertson Jr. Together they served the church during its first 28 years of existence.

In 1830 the site for a church building was selected by Elder Robertson, and a committee, composed of James Reddick, James Jolly, and Amos McLemore, was appointed to oversee construction. The structure was to be 30 feet by 24 feet, built of hewn logs with a plank floor and shingle roof. Notes from the 100th anniversary celebration record that their first structure stood until 1858 when a new building was complete...Minutes of May 1859 state that the new building was then ready to be occupied...A 1940 structure was built approximately six miles east of Collins, Mississippi, off Highway 84E, and known today as the Leaf River Baptist Church.

In December 1838 Elizabeth Rogers died and was buried in the family cemetery on Meshack's property. In 1839 Meshack married Mary Lucretia Geiger who was born on May 20, 1816, in Collins, Covington County, Mississippi. Meshack and Lucretia had five more children:

Elizabeth Lucy Rogers was born on September 13, 1841;
Mary "Polly" Rogers was born May 29, 1844, and died in 1881;
Meshack, Jr., was born on January 29, 1847, and died in 1927;
George Washington Rogers was born on May 1, 1849, and died in 1921;
Charity Tobitha Rogers was born June 9, 1851, and died in 1887.

Six of Meshack's children married Duckworth girls, and one girl married a Speed son. The Duckworth and Speed families were prominent families in the Leaf River Baptist Church and in the surrounding community. The Rogers children and spouses are listed below:

Sarah married James Monroe Speed;
Elizabeth married Charles C. Carter;
Caroline married 1) George Benjamin Duckworth and 2) Jackson Edmondson;

Shadrack married 1) Mary Duckworth and 2) Martha A. Goss;
Josiah Rogers married Kisiah Duckworth;
Timothy Luther married 1) Sarah Elizabeth (Betsie) Duckworth
   and 2) Rachel Rebecca Duckworth;
Norvell married 1) Frances Caroline Duckworth and 2) Rachel
   Mathison;
Martha married James West;
George Benjamin married Hester Duckworth;
William married Mary Jane West.

As indicated earlier, Meshack bought significant land in Covington County, Mississippi. In 1841 he received an additional land grant for 79.57 acres from the Federal government signed by President Martin Van Buren.

In the 1850 census, Meshack was listed as 54 years of age, a farmer by occupation, with a real estate value of $240. By the 1860 census his real estate was valued at $2,000 plus a personal property of $15,000.

Lucertia Rogers died in December 1854, and Meshack married once again. His third wife was Caroline Campbell Purvis, who was born on January 30, 1810, in Pendleton, Anderson District, South Carolina. They had no children together.

The Civil War struck hard in Mississippi, and like all the other farmers in the area, Meshack's estate decreased significantly. In the 1870 census, Meshack's third wife, Caroline, held "real estate valued at $160 and personal property at just $600." [Information from Anne Eiland] In addition to financial loss, the Meshack Rogers family suffered the loss of many sons and relatives.

Meshack Rogers died in Covington County in December of 1869 and was buried in the Meshack Rogers Cemetery on his property. He was the father of fifteen children and had ninety grandchildren at his death! [Anne Eiland].

Josiah Rogers:

The son of Meshack Rogers and Elizabeth Lucy Brunson, Josiah Rogers was born in Williamsburg, Covington County, Mississippi, on January 19, 1827. He was the second of eight sons born to Meshack, and he grew up on his father's farm. He most likely attended Leaf River Baptist Church and enjoyed the social activities of the congregation. There he met and married Kisiah Duckworth, the daughter of Zabud Duckworth and Mary Jane (Polly) Thompson, who were also active members of the church. Josiah and Kisiah married on January 4, 1848.

To this family were born two children, as listed on the 1850 Federal Census of Covington County: **Mary Malissa** (born April 12, 1849) and Joseph Timothy (born April 24, 1850). By the 1860 census, their family had grown to include the following offspring:

Benjamin Meshack, born March 23, 1851;
Charity Elizabeth, born April 27, 1853, and died in April 1922 in
    Forrest, Mississippi;
Daniel Caniday, born April 26, 1854;
Zabud Alonzo, born on July 24, 1855, and married his sister's
    step-daughter, Sara McDonald Byrd, on December 23, 1866,
    and died on November 20, 1929;
Arthur LaFayette, born on April 8, 1857, and died in July 1909;
Josiah Brunson, born June 10, 1858;
Lucy Keziah, born September 27, 1859.

In the 1860 census, Josiah was listed as a farmer with real estate valued at $2,000 and personal property at $2,500.

According to Anne Eiland, "When the call came for volunteers for the Confederate Army (CSA) in Covington County, Josiah, along with four brothers (Shadrack, Timothy, Norvell Marion, and Benjamin) went to Williamsburg, the county seat, to enlist in Company B, Mississippi Volunteers, which was being organized by Captain T. D. Magee. There was said to have been some 200 volunteers, including several Duckworth brothers-in-law, nephews, and others from the area. The 6th (Balfour's) Battalion Mississippi Infantry was not formerly organized until about April of 1862. [It was later increased and reorganized into a regiment and its designation changed to the 46th Regiment Mississippi Infantry by S. O. No. 32, Hd. Qrs. 2d District, Dept. M and E La, dated Vicksburg, December 2, 1862].

The volunteers marched from Williamsburg amid a local celebration following a "volunteers farewell celebration held by their families and the community with a picnic of chicken pie, biscuits, corn bread, barbecued beef, mutton, and boiled pork hams…" according to an account recorded by Elsie Posey, who was present. It is not clear, from the available military records, exactly what date Josiah was *officially* enlisted. It is thought that he signed up at the same time as the others, which would have been in February of 1862, but a confusion in the spelling of his name (Rodgers for Rogers) left the records unclear. The earliest muster records found, that contained his name, were dated February 16, 1863, and that date was assigned as his enlistment date. [Information from Anne Eiland and from *Covington Crossroads*, page 73].

Josiah was involved in the following Civil War campaigns:

Chickasaw Bayou (Grant's Operations against Vicksburg) December 26-29, 1862: On December 26, 1862, three Union divisions, under Major General William T. Sherman, disembarked at Johnson's Plantation on the Yazoo River to approach the Vicksburg defenses from the northeast while a fourth landed farther upstream on December 27. The Federals pushed their lines forward through the swamps toward Walnut Hills, which were strongly defended. On the 28th, several futile attempts were made to get around these defenses, and on December 29, Sherman ordered a frontal assault which was repulsed by the Confederates (including the 46th Mississippi) and left the Union Army with heavy casualties. Sherman then withdrew. This Confederate victory frustrated Grant's attempts to take Vicksburg by direct approach.

Battle of Port Gibson (Grant's Operations against Vicksburg) May 1, 1863: Major General U. S. Grant launched his march on Vicksburg in the spring of 1863, starting his army south from Milliken's Bend which was on the west side of the Mississippi River. He intended to cross the river at Grand Gulf, but the Union fleet was unable to silence the Confederate big guns there. Grant then marched farther south and crossed at Bruinsburg on April 30. His army came ashore, secured the landing area, and by late afternoon, began marching inland. Advancing on the Rodney Road towards Port Gibson, the Union forces ran into Rebel outposts after midnight and skirmished with them for around three hours. After 3:00 a.m. the fighting stopped. At dawn, Grant advanced his men along the Rodney Road and on a plantation road. At 5:30 a.m. the Confederates attacked the Union advance and the battle ensued. The Confederates were forced to fall back and establish new defensive positions at different times during the day, but they could not stop the Union onslaught and were forced to leave the field in the early evening after suffering 787 casualties. The 46th served under Brig. General John S. Bowen during this engagement.

<u>Battle of Vicksburg</u> June 18-July 4, 1863: The 46th saw battle action throughout the spring and summer of 1863 in the battle for Vicksburg, including the siege of Vicksburg itself. Major General Ulysses S. Grant's armies converged on Vicksburg, invading the city and entrapping a Confederate army under Lt. Gen. John Pemberton. After a prolonged siege, the city surrendered. When Vicksburg fell on July 4, 1863, Josiah and his brothers, Norvell and Timothy, along with the Duckworths, were among those who signed the oath of surrender. Josiah signed on July 8, 1863, and for reasons known only to him, Josiah signed his name "Rodgers" rather than "Rogers." [Would this have enabled him to join the Confederate army later under the name of "Rogers"?] Following the surrender, the 46th Battalion was disorganized and placed on parole furlough. (Josiah's brother, Benjamin, had died at Camp Tupelo on July 15, 1862, of intermittent fever.) Neither Josiah nor Joseph Duckworth was counted as *present* on the prisoner muster list on August 23, 1863, and were noted *absent without leave*. They had already left to walk home to Covington County. The 46th Battalion was not formerly *exchanged* until October 16, 1863, some three months after the surrender.

<u>Reorganization</u>: Members of the 46th began reporting back to their Battalion in November 1863. Major Constantine Rea, of the 46th Regiment Mississippi Infantry, formed what was called "Rea's Battalion of Sharp Shooters" in February 1864, as directed by CSA Field authorities. Since the 46th had been officially *disorganized* and *surrendered* following the Fall of Vicksburg, this new group was considered a *temporary organization* and apparently not given official recognition in writing by the Confederate War Department. However, they were assigned to the Army of Tennessee and sent to Georgia.

<u>Battle of New Hope</u> (Atlanta Campaign) May 25-26, 1864: After General Joseph E. Johnston of the Army of Tennessee, CSA, retreated to Allatoona Pass on May 19-20, 1864, Sherman decided that he would most likely pay dearly for attacking Johnston there, so he chose to move around Johnston's left flank and steal a march toward Dallas, Georgia. Johnston anticipated Sherman's move and met the Union forces at New Hope Church. Sherman mistakenly surmised that Johnston had a token force at New Hope and ordered Major General Joseph Hooker's corps to attack. This corps was severely mauled. On the 26th of May, both sides were entrenched and skirmishing continued throughout the day. Josiah was wounded in the shoulder either on the 25th or 26th during this battle. [Kisiah later told her grandchildren that she saw her husband Josiah, who was away fighting, come around the house with his saddle on his back.

She later learned that this would have been the same day, during the Battle of New Hope, that his horse had been shot out from under him and he had been wounded.]

Badly wounded, Josiah set out for Mississippi, walking all the way, only to die at home on June 28 from infection and blood poisoning from his wounds. He was only 37 years old! His body was interred in the Meshack Rogers Cemetery, and two markers were placed on his grave site—one for his body and one to his memory.

Three more children were born to Josiah and Kisiah Rogers:

> Augustus Columbus Rogers was born on January 29, 1861, before Josiah enlisted; died in 1893;

> Norval Dolberry [sometimes spelled Doleberry] Rogers, born May 14, 1862, before Josiah left for the Vicksburg Campaign; died on August 8, 1944; [Note: One of Norval Doleberry Rogers' sons, Rufus Rogers was a contemporary and friend of the children of James Edward Byrd]

> John William Rogers, born August 16, 1864, two months after his father's death; died in 1935.

The 1870 Federal Census for Covington County shows Kisiah living alone with eleven children. Now their real estate was valued at $320 and personal property at $500. The war had cost the Rogers' family dearly. Kisiah was a charter member of Salem Baptist Church and taught her children to love the Lord despite the deprivation they all felt.

In the 1900 Census Kisiah was living with her son, John William Rogers and his wife Kate. As a war widow, Kisiah filed a pension application on August 30, 1907, for a Military Pension for Josiah's service in the CSA.

Kisiah Duckworth Rogers died on February 20, 1910. She was apparently a dutiful wife, a cherished mother, a hard worker, and a devout Christian. At the time of her death, the pastor of Rock Hill Baptist Church wrote this obituary:

> On November 1, 1827, God gave to Mr. and Mrs. Zarbard (sic) Duckworth of South Carolina a jewel of the rarest hue. Early in life this daughter was brought to Mississippi.

On January 4, 1848 she was married to Josiah Rogers. To this union God gave nine sons and three daughters. From the wound received during the Civil War, Mr. Rogers was laid to rest with the Boys in Gray, thus leaving her to brave the dangers and undergo the difficulties of widow and orphan, but the difficulties were met and overcome and today all except two boys await the call to which mother answered February 20, 1910. As noble a body of high-toned Christian citizens as this country affords, all members of a Baptist church and four of the men are Deacon. This is but the result of over sixty years of faithful service in the Kingdom of God.

Mrs. Rogers' memorial cannot be obtained by pen, tongue or brush, but abides in themselves blessed by her kind words, golden deeds, untiring energy and motherly influence. May God give to this world more such mothers in Israel. On February the 21st amid sobs and signs [sic] of a tremendous congregation, she was laid to rest in Rock Hill Cemetery. Peace to her memory until the angels awake her in the morning of the resurrection.

The local newspaper ran this obituary under the title of *Noble Mother Gone*:

Mrs. Keziah [sic] Rogers was born in South Carolina, November 1st, 1827. She came with her father, Zabral [sic] Duckworth, to Mississippi when quite a child. She was married to Josiah Rogers, January 4th, 1848. To them were born nine sons and three daughters. All the children grew to manhood and womanhood. Seven sons and three daughters survive her.

In the death of Mrs. Rogers, the community gives up one of the noble women and one of the best mothers the county has ever known. She was an earnest Christian, having been a member of the Baptist church for sixty years. Her husband gave his life to his country, dying of a wound received in the Civil War. Some estimate of her life may be realized, when we think how she provided for her large family of children and reared them in such a way that it was even a marvel to her neighbors. Her children have all made high-toned Christian characters. They stand among the foremost citizens in the communities where they live and can always be found ready to stand on the right side of every moral question. Four of her sons are deacons in Baptist churches. She indeed fought a good fight and has now gone to her reward.

Mary Malissa [Sometimes spelled Melissa] Rogers:

Not much is known about the childhood of Malissa Rogers, but since she was the oldest child of Josiah and Kisiah Rogers, she probably spent a lot of time helping her mother in the house. She was about thirteen years old when her father left home to serve in the Confederate army; and being a girl, she most likely helped with the cooking, cleaning, and tending to younger siblings. There were eight younger siblings in the home, and the family lived on a farm. There was plenty of work to be done by the children while their father was gone. According to Gwen Keys Hitt in *Covington Crossroads* [pages 73-74):

> The War was a total war. Not only were soldiers fighting, but their families were fighting as well. Women, children, old men, and slaves were left to take on the responsibility of carrying on life as best they could...The cornmeal was sifted and the bran browned and used as coffee...Soda was gotten from the ashes of burning corn cobs...Dye was made from walnut bank, hickory nut bark, and berry juices. Candles were made from tallow and beeswax and substituted for coal oil and kerosene...The women continued to weave the cloth from the home-grown cotton and then to make the clothes for the whole family, including the soldiers...by hand...Those at home tried to keep the farms in operation, but this became increasingly difficult.

The family were active members of Leaf River Baptist Church, and after the Civil War, Malissa met (or at least became re-acquainted with) John King Byrd. A courtship began and the two were married on Christmas Eve in 1867. He was thirty-four years old and she was eighteen.

The couple moved to the Byrd family farm near Burton's Creek, and lived with King's father, Jack Byrd. Their first son was born on May 10, 1872, and they named him James Edward [probably named for King's two uncles]. They subsequently had seven more children: three more sons and four daughters. Malissa named her first daughter, Charity Elizabeth, the name of Malissa's sister, and another daughter Mary Keziah [named for Mary's two grandmothers]. In addition to James Edward, there was

John King, Jr., Archie Fairley [named for King's commanding officer in the Civil War], and Josiah Brunson [named for his maternal grandfather].

King Byrd suffered from a war wound the rest of his life which might have kept him from being active in church. At any rate, Malissa Roger was a charter member of the Rock Hill Baptist Church, established on land donated by J. King Byrd. Their son, James Edward, was the first Sunday School superintendent of that church.

Malissa lived a long, productive life and died in 1921 at age 72. She was buried in the Rock Hill Baptist Church cemetery. The following is her obituary [which also appears in *Traveling Companions* by this author]:

> Mrs. Mary Malissa Byrd, wrought well through life's day, as the oldest of a family of twelve children; as a faithful wife, and sacrificing, untiring mother of four sons and four daughters, including our honored Secretary of Sunday School work [Dr. James Edward Byrd]; and as a loyal member of Rock Hill church. Just nine days beyond the seventy-second milestone, she fell asleep and many of her friends gathered at her church to see her off on her journey to heaven, tucked beneath a quilt of clay and a coverlet of flowers. One word with its full significance tells her life story—mother...

Mary Malissa Rogers married into the Byrd family, becoming the mother of James Edward Byrd, who was the father of Edward Leavell Byrd; and who, in turn, was the father of Hersey Davis Byrd. Thus ends the story of the Rogers Family and how it is related to the Byrd Family.

Sources:

Shadrach and Hopey Rogers and Families by William Morgan Brown
    (Decorah, Iowa: Anundsen Publishing Company, 2007);
Rogers-Rodgers: Westward from the Carolinas by William Morgan Brown
    (Decorah, Iowa: Anundsen Publishing Company, 1996);
Covington Crossroads by Gwen Keys Hitt (Hattiesburg: University of
Southern Mississippi Printing Center, 1985);
Goodspeed's Biographical and Historical Memoirs of Mississippi, Vol. 11,
Published in 1891;
1790, 1800, 1810 U. S Census;
https://www.ancestry.com/imageviewer/collections/12543/images/dvm_
dez_GenMono001765-00061-1?ssrc=&backlabel=Return&pId=100;
https://en.wikipedia.org/wiki/John_Rogers_(Bible_editor_and_martyr;
https://en.wikipedia.org/wiki/Thomas_Rogers_(Mayflower_passenger);
bumsteadsr@hotmail.com;
https://www.facebook.com/ShadrackRogers/posts/shadrach-shadrack-
rogersca-1750-ca-1828-our-chapter-is-named-for-shadrach-
rogers/417622444938667/;
Archives of the University of Southern Mississippi, Manuscript Collection:
    Leaf River Baptist Church Minutes;
Letters and Papers Belonging to the Family of J. E. Byrd;
Personal Visits to Covington and Simpson Counties, Mississippi, sites;
Dillon
    and Marion Counties, South Carolina, sites;
Various Web Searches:
Ancestry.com;
Genealogy.com;
RootsWeb.com;
Google Searches;
Newspaper Articles in the *News-Commercial*, Collins, Mississippi;
Anne Eiland, Scottsdale, Arizona: Aeiland0218@yahoo.com.

THE THOMPSON FAMILY

How does the Thompson family relate to the Byrd family?

Mary "Polly" Jane Thompson married Zabud Duckworth. Their daughter was Kisiah Duckworth, who married Josiah Rogers. Josiah and Kisiah were the parents of Mary Malissa Rogers, who married John King Byrd. Their son was James Edward Byrd, the father of Edward Leavell Byrd. Edward's son was Hersey Davis Byrd.

Joseph Thompson:

Mary Jane Thompson was the daughter of Joseph Thompson, from the Pendleton District of upcountry South Carolina. Records for these early settlers are hard to find. Some say Joseph Thompson was born on a ship on its way from England to the American colonies. Some say it was on a ship that Joseph Thompson married his wife. Suffice it to say, he was English and arrived in America before the Revolutionary War. His date of birth was 1749.

There are records of a Moses Thompson who lived in Virginia, and some researchers feel he was the father of Joseph Thompson. However, the will of Moses Thompson indicates he was living in the Charleston area at the time of his death, and there is no mention of Joseph. This may mean that Joseph was not part of this family, or it could mean he had moved to upper South Carolina and was no longer in touch with the family when the father died.

Some researchers have also added the middle name of Patrick to the elder Joseph Thompson, and the middle name of Robert to his son, also named Joseph Thompson. Definitive documentation of these names has not been located.

Joseph married Mary "Molly" Jolly (who was also born in 1749) in January 1769. There were several Jolly families in the Pendleton District in the early days before the Revolutionary War. It is unclear to which family Molly was related.

During the Revolutionary War, Joseph Thompson was a "forage master," which means he basically hunted supplies of feed for the animals and food for the soldiers. A record from "Selected Virginia Revolutionary War Records, Volume 1" shows that Joseph Thompson received eighteen pounds for hay and subsistence. He was in Caroline County, Virginia, when he served as a forage master, but it is unknown if he was in the area because of the Patriot army or if he was actually living there.

In addition to his service as a part-time forage master, Joseph Thompson served as a lieutenant in the First or Southern Battalion of Militia of Orange County, North Carolina, under the command of Colonel Albrose Ramsey, Major Hugh Tinnian, and Captain William Williams. While he was away with the militia, "his wife and children hid in a cave for two days because there was a price on her head for carrying information to the Patriots." After the war Joseph (or possibly his son by the same name) filed for claims for land in South Carolina.
[Source: *Thompson Genealogical Journal*, posted on Ancestry.com by Jay Gatewood, June 4, 2012]

Joseph and Molly were the parents of the following children, all of whom were born in South Carolina:

Joseph Thompson, Jr., born 1774 and died about 1880 in
    Forsyth, Georgia;
Robert Thompson, born 1776 and died after 1850 in
    Carroll County, Georgia;
Randsom Thompson, born 1778 and died on July 3, 1843 in
    Carroll County, Georgia;
Elizabeth "Betsy" Thompson, born 1780, married Thomas
    Garner, and died in 1849 in Haralson, Georgia;
Nancy Thompson, born 1781 and married first Isham Green
    and then Laudwick Orr, a minister, and died about 1870 in
    Cleburne County, Alabama;
Zachariah Thompson, born 1788, and died September 23,
    1868 in Jasper County, Mississippi;
Rebecca Jane Thompson, born September 18, 1793 and
    married John L. Hunnicutt, and died on October 31, 1884,
    in Cleburne County, Alabama;
John David Thompson, born 1795; date of death unknown;
Mary Jane Thompson, born February 5, 1803, married
    Zabud Duckworth, and died on February 28, 1883, in
    Covington County, Mississippi.

Joseph died in 1810, but his cause of death and place of burial are unknown. In his will, dated October 9, 1810, he left each child five shillings and anything that was leftover was to be given to his wife who was named as executrix. Robert Thompson was listed as executor of the will.

When Joseph died, John David was only fifteen and Mary Jane was seven. They lived with their mother, Molly, for a while, and then Molly moved in with her daughter Rebecca, who had married John Hunnicutt. Sometime in the early 1830s the Hunnicutts moved to Alabama, and Molly moved with them. Mother Molly lived to be about 100 years old [assuming the date of her birth is correct] and was buried in the Old Campground Cemetery in Cleburne County, Alabama. Her grave is not marked.

[Note: An interesting "aside" or "Pioneer Tidbit..." from William Morgan Brown, the author of several genealogy books, including information on the Thompson family:

> Did you know that our pioneer ancestors did not have beautiful yards around their homes like we do today? Many of their homes were built in the midst of cane breaks and dense woods. 'Early to bed' had a different connotation: They got into their beds while it was light enough to check their bedding for sneaky snakes. Snakes would crawl into their homes during early evening when the cool temperatures were settling into the woods. Early log homes did not have windows, so snakes had easy access to nice, warm bedding.

Mary Jane "Polly" Thompson:

Polly Thompson was the youngest child of Joseph and Molly Thompson and was born on February 5, 1803 [the year of the Louisiana Purchase by Thomas Jefferson].

She was only seven years old when her father died in South Carolina, but she remained in the home with her mother. In June 1819 at the age of sixteen she married Zabud (Zabard) Franklin Duckworth, who was born in Anson County, North Carolina, on April 28, 1792. He would have been 27 when they married.

They were the parents of fourteen children, six of whom were born in the Pendleton District of South Carolina. The rest were born in Covington County, Mississippi. [Note: The list of these children also appears in the chapter on the Duckworth family.]

George Benjamin, 1820, married Nancy Caroline Rogers;
   died in 1865 in Covington County;
Ellender, October 18, 1822, married Benjamin Robert Speed,
   died on December 21, 1896 in Fairfield, Freestone County,
   Texas;
Mary "Polly," April 21, 1824, married Shadrack Rogers, and
   died January 11, 1884 in Oden, Montgomery, Arkansas;
Sarah Elizabeth "Betsie," October 20, 1825, married Timothy
   Luther Rogers; died August 13, 1864 in Covington County
   in childbirth;
Kisiah, November 1, 1827, married Josiah Rogers; died
   February 20, 1810, in Covington County;
Charity Pamelia, April 19, 1828, married Benjamin Rawls, III,
   died on September 8, 1904 in Lamar County, Mississippi;
Frances Caroline, December 25, 1830 in Covington County,
   married Marion Norvell Rogers, died October 17, 1861, in
   Covington County;
Joseph Thompson, August 13, 1832 in Covington County;
   married Martha "Mary" Jane Speed, died on March 4, 1887,
   Covington County;
Daniel James, 1834 in Covington County, died in 1863, in a
   Civil War battle;
Hester Jane, November 25, 1835 in Covington County,
   married George Benjamin Rogers, died on July 11, 1899, in
   Long Leaf, Louisiana;
Nancy Caroline, July 17, 1837 in Covington County, married
   Meshack Rogers, Jr., died on December 28, 1927, in
   Covington County;
Rachel Rebecca, November 10, 1838, in Covington County,
   married Timothy Luther Rogers, died on August 3, 1926,
   in Covington County;
Bronson David, November 10, 1840, in Covington County,
   died on January 5, 1863, in the Battle of Stones River in
   Murfreesboro, Tennessee, during the Civil War;
Zabard, Franklin., Jr., 1842, in Covington County, died in Lamar
   County, Georgia, during the Civil War.

The Civil War was not kind to Polly Thompson. Her husband died at age 71 in the midst of the conflict. She lost four sons and two sons-in-law, either in the war itself or as a result of the war. One daughter died in childbirth, and two sons-in-law were captured in the Battle of Vicksburg by the Yankees, but both survived. One son and four sons-in-law fought for the Confederacy and survived the war. It is hard to imagine the pain and suffering of this Duckworth family.

Polly herself lived twenty years after the death of Zabud. She was eighty years old and had probably lived with some of her children. The family were active members of Leaf River Baptist Church where Zabud and Polly were buried.

Kisiah Duckworth Rogers and Descendants:

Kisiah was born in South Carolina, but moved with her family to Mississippi where she met and married Josiah Rogers. [More information on this family can be found in the Rogers family chapter.]

Kisiah's first child was Mary Malissa Rogers who married John King Byrd, and their story can be found in the book, *Traveling Companions,* by this author and also in the Rogers family chapter. Of their eight children, the oldest son was James Edward Byrd who married Effie Leona McNeil. [More information on Leona can be found in the McNeil family chapter.]

James Edward and Effie also had eight children, but the first son was stillborn. They had four daughters before their first son was born, and they named him Edward Leavell Byrd.

Edward was a Baptist minister who married Nora Beatrice Brown. [More information on Nora can be found in the Brown family chapter]. They had three children, and the second son was Hersey Davis Byrd.

This concludes the linkage between the Thompson family and the Byrd family, who have acknowledged that they come from "good stock." The Thompson/Duckworth family were early settlers of Mississippi and carved a heritage that the Byrd family is proud to call their own.

Sources:

Rogers-Rodgers: Westward from the Carolinas by William Morgan Brown (Decorah, Iowa: Anundsen Publishing Company, 1996);
Google Searches: "Moses Thompson, Joseph Thompson"
Thompson Genealogical Journal, posted on Ancestry.com by Jay Gatewood, June 4, 2012
Internet:
  Ancestry.com
  Geni.com
  Genealogy.com
  Genealogy Trails.com
  Mitchellfarms.com
  Roster of 46th Mississippi Infantry, Company B, Civil War
  FamilySearch.com
Family Information

Kay Byrd

THE WESSINGER FAMILY

How does the Wessinger family relate to the Byrd family?
Anna Barbara Wessinger married Michael Eargle, Jr. They were the parents of Christian Eargle who married James McNure. The son of Christian and James McNure was Henry Adam David McNure/McNeil. David McNeil married Sarah Caroline McLaurin, and their daughter was Effie Leona McNeil who married James Edward Byrd, the father of Edward Leavell Byrd. Edward's son was Hersey Davis Byrd.

Matthias Wessinger was born Matthaus Wossinger on April 20, 1723, in Darmsbach, Landkreis Engkreis, Wurttemberg, Germany. He was the son of Matthes Wossinger, and he married Margaretha Siebler on January 9, 1744. Margaretha was the daughter of Adam Siebler and Margaretha Rosswag, and she was born on December 17, 1719.

Mathias and Margaretha were the parents of Johann Michael Wessinger, Mathias Wessinger, Jr., and Anna Catharina Wessinger. Mathias worked as a cowherd in Nottingen, and they lived in an area of southern Germany which was besieged by warring armies during the Thirty Years' War. Their crops were destroyed or seized by the armies, they worked as serfs for an overlord, and their Protestant religion was in constant conflict with the predominately Catholic Church.
[Source: http://dutchforkchapter.org/auswanderer_early.html

When agents from America visited the area and offered enticing lands in the New World, these poor people were attracted.

> Between the years 1730 and 1766 the colonial government of South Carolina actively encouraged immigration of foreign Protestants to the Province. Appreciable numbers of immigrants from Germany [and German areas in Switzerland] began to arrive in the 1740s. The year 1752 represented the peak of the migration with about 1,800 German settlers who arrived on several ships in the fall of that year. Saxe-Gotha, Amelia, Salkehatchie, and the fork of the Broad and Saluda Rivers (Dutch Fork) became predominately German settlements. The Dutch Fork was the most densely settled, becoming home to 483 settler families by 1760, almost all of whom were of German origin..."
> [Source: www.dutchforkchapter.org]

Mathias was released from bonded serfdom and granted a right to emigrate to America on February 16, 1752. The Wessingers were part of this German migration arriving in Charleston harbor in 1752 from the Palatinate area of Germany. Like most German settlers, they applied for a state land grant, petitioning for 150 acres of land on Rawls Creek in the Dutch Fork. It was granted on April 3, 1772.
[Source: www.wikitree.com/wiki/Wessinger-32]

Mathias and Margaret were active members of the Dutch Fork community. He built a home, worked their land, and the whole family worshipped God as Lutherans.

In 1757 another child was born into the family, and he was named John Jacob Wessinger. Now their family consisted of the following children:

Johan Michael Wessinger, born on May 2, 1744, in Wurttemberg, Germany and died in Calhoun County, Arkansas. He married Margaret Elizabeth [Schmidt] Smith in 1774 in Lexington County, South Carolina.

Mathias Wessinger, Jr., was born on March 22, 1746, in Wurttemberg, Germany. [More on this son later.]

Anna Catherina Wessinger, born on April 9, 1751 in Wurttemberg, Germany. She married John Kleckley in 1773, who was also born in Wurttemberg, Germany, although they did not marry until later years in South Carolina. Both died in 1820 and were buried in South Carolina.

Cathrina was captured by Indians in the Saxa-Gotha area, SC. She impressed the Indians with her courage, refused to cower, and escaped after several months' captivity circa 1773. An interesting descendant of Catherina Wessinger was First Lady Roslyn Carter!
[Source: Ancestry.com Posted by francesCHall16248; viewer/tree/66102182/person/382204428591/media/448 c88ca-b895-470d-bcc7-2dfeb781c32f?usePUBJs=true]

John Jacob Wessinger, born about 1757 and died about 1809 in South Carolina. He was married first to Rachel Shuler and secondly to Susannah (surname unknown). He had one son and three daughters according to the U. S. Census of 1790. He was buried not far from Beard's Creek, near the property of his brother Mathias Wessinger, Jr.

Both Mathias and Margaret died and were buried in South Carolina, although their graves were presumably covered by Lake Murray in later years.

Mathias Wessinger, Jr.

Mathias Wessinger, Jr., was six years old when he accompanied his family on the Ship Rowand to America. Among the other passengers on the ship were the Sieblers, the Schmidts and other German-speaking families.

Mathias married Lydia Anna Schmidt [Smith] on October 2, 1771, apparently in the Dutch Fork community. They had seven children:

1. Uriah George Wessinger, born 1771, married Elizabeth Derrick, and died on October 3, 1846, in Lexington County, South Carolina;
2. Mathias Wessinger, III, born in 1774, married Elizabeth Koon, died September 20, 1841, in South Carolina;
3. Catherine Wessinger, born in 1776 and died on September 13, 1835, in South Carolina;
4. Anna Barbara Wessinger, born 1778 in South Carolina, and married Michael Eargle, died in South Carolina in 1845;
5. Mary Magdalene Wessinger, born about 1780, married Joseph Lybrand, and died on October 8, 1872, in South Carolina;
6. George Wessinger was born about 1784. No further information is available. It is assumed he lived and died in South Carolina;
7. Anna Wessinger, born 1786, married John Koon, and died in 1845, in Lexington County, South Carolina.

Mathias' father-in-law was John Ulrich Smith and he had a 200-acre land grant which was willed to Mathias upon the death of John Smith. This land was located on the west side of High Hill Creek. Upon this land Mathias and Anna made their home and, when they died, they along with six of their children were buried on this land. Mathias died on March 27, 1816, but the death of Anna is unknown.

One internet researcher wrote: "He was buried in High Hill Church [cemetery], near his home, just below Dr. Wessinger's old place."

[Source: rootsweb.com; www.wikitree.com/wiki/Wessinger-32; CountryGirlxxxxv@aol.com, RootsWeb.com]

Another source says the Wessingers were buried in Wessinger Cemetery. Whichever place they were buried, their graves now lie under Lake Murray. [Source: Ancestry.com posted by subseti1]

Anna Barbara Wessinger

Anna Barbara was born in the Dutch Fork community among many German-speaking people. There she met and married Michael Eargle. They were parents of the following children:

Nancy Eargle was born about 1802, married John Slice, the son of Uriah Slice and the brother of Elias Slice. She died in July 1896.

Margaret Catherine Eargle was born on September 28, 1802. She married Joshua Taylor (1809-1880), the son of Jonathan Taylor and Rachel Clark, on February 5, 1837. Margaret died on October 29, 1886, and is buried alongside her husband in the Boiling Springs Methodist Church cemetery in Lexington County, South Carolina.

Mary Magdalena Eargle was born about 1803 and married Elias Slice, the brother of her sister's husband.

Rebecca Eargle was born in 1810 and married David Derrick, the son of Andrew Derrick and Catherine Hiller. Rebecca and David Derrick are buried in the Derrick Cemetery, Lake Murray.

Christian (sometimes spelled Christina) Eargle was born about 1811 and married James McNure, born about 1803. [More about this person follows.]

David Eargle was born in 1814 and married Mary Magdalene Wessinger, the daughter of Uriah Wessinger and Elizabeth Derrick. He died about 1850.

Sally Eargle, born about 1816, married Jeremiah "Jesse" Miller, the son of Henry Mill and Permelia Taylor. She died on December 12, 1876.

Mary Barbara Eargle, born about 1817, married Levi Shealy on December 7, 1837. He was born on April 14, 1816 and was the son of John Ventle Shealy and Eva Margaret Sease.

Anna Barbara Wessinger died in 1845 in South Carolina.

Christian (or Christina) Eargle

Although Christian lived in the Dutch Fork community and was around German-speaking people all the time, she was swept off her feet by James McNure with a Scottish background. They were married some time before 1839 and were the parents of five children:

Martha E. McNure, born in 1839;
Henry Adam David McNure, born in 1841;
Mary McNure, born in 1843;
George W. McNure, born in 1845;
Louisa "Lou" McNure, born in 1849.

[Note: More information on this family can be found in the chapter entitled The McNeil Family.]

The family remained in the Columbia, South Carolina, area until some time prior to the Civil War when they moved to Smith County, Mississippi. They were listed on the Mississippi Census in 1866, and James McNure also bought land in Smith County in 1866.

In 1870 James McNure was on the U.S. Census at age 72 and Christian was listed as 62 years old. By 1880 James McNure had died. Christian was identified as a widow on the census, and she was living with her son H.A.D. McNeil and his wife Sarah Caroline. The date of her death is unknown.

Henry Adam David McNure/McNeil

David McNure changed his name after the Civil War to honor his Confederate commanding officer, Lt.Col. Adin McNeill, with the blessings of the McNeil family. He married Sarah Caroline McLaurin, and they were the parents of Effie Leona McNeil. Effie married James Edward Byrd and they were the parents of Edward Leavell Byrd, who was the father of Hersey Davis Byrd.

Sources:

Websites:
www.dutchforkchapter.org
http://dutchforkchapter.org/auswanderer_early.html
Ancestry.com:
    francesCHall16248.
    viewer/tree/66102182/person/382204428591/media/448c88ca-
    b895-470d-bcc7-2dfeb781c32f?usePUBJs=true
www.wikitree.com/wiki/Wessinger-32;CountryGirlxxxxv@aol.com,
RootsWeb.com
https://www.geni.com/people/John-Weisinger-Sr/6000000009754650774
Mississippi Census 1866
U.S. Census 1870, 1880

THE WHITEHEAD FAMILY

How does the Whitehead Family relate to the Byrd Family?
Elizabeth (Betsey) Whitehead married Jack W. Byrd and was the mother of John King Byrd who was the grandfather of Edward Leavell Byrd. Edward Byrd was the father of Hersey Davis Byrd.

There is very little information on Elizabeth (Betsey) Whitehead's family on the Internet or in family papers. According to the 1830 US Census, she was living in Rankin County, Mississippi. Her date of birth seems to be 1800 (or 1803) and place of birth is somewhere in Georgia.

Nita Byrd Lumpkin met a distant cousin and a descendant of the Whitehead family, Kate Whitehead Caskey. Kate was kind enough to share some family history with Nita. She said that Betsey's parents were James Whitehead, Sr., and Charity West (or Wiggins). James Whitehead was born about 1755 but his place of birth is unknown. Charity was several years younger than James but no other information is available for her.

Their children were:

John Whitehead, born on March 6, 1790, in Georgia, lived in Rankin County, Mississippi, and died in 1860 in Covington County, Mississippi;

Elizabeth (Betsey) Whitehead, born in Georgia about 1803; married Jack W. Byrd on January 24, 1832, and died in Mississippi;

Martha Ann, born in 1804 in Georgia, married Arthur Guy (or Gay), and died on March 3, 1898, in Tunnel Hill, Lauderdale County, Mississippi;

James Whitehead, Jr., born between 1800 and 1810 in Georgia and died in Lauderdale County, Mississippi in 1842.
[Source: laurene777@yahoo.com via Nita Byrd Lumpkin]

An internet search revealed that a man named James Whitehead lived in the Mississippi Territory in 1805, 1810, and 1818. Kate Whitehead Caskey noted that James Whitehead served in the Revolutionary War, and an entry in Ancestry.com shows that James Whitehead was a Second Lieutenant in "2 (Fitzpatrick's) Regiment, Mississippi Territory Militia" in

the Revolutionary War. In addition, the Census of Pensioners Revolutionary or Military Services taken in 1840 lists James Whitehead as living in Lauderdale County, Mississippi. He was 85 years old and living with James Whitehead, the "name of the head of families with whom pensioners resided on June 1, 1840."
[Source: ancestry.com: U.S. Compiled Service Records, Post-Revolutionary War Volunteer Soldiers, 1784-1811 for James Whitehead and Census of Pensioners, Mississippi – Southern District]

As stated above, James and Charity lived with their son James, Jr., and his wife, Margaret Graham Whitehead. In 1840 there were three children also living in the household. Even though James, Jr., was probably a farmer/planter, there was no mention of slaves living in the Whitehead household.

James, Sr., and Charity, as well as their son James, Jr., died in 1842 and were buried in the Graham Cemetery in Lauderdale County, Mississippi. Kate Caskey speculates that some sort of epidemic must have occurred in the Lauderdale County area which took their lives.
[Source: robert.e.caskey@gte.net via Nita Byrd Lumpkin]

John Whitehead married Dorcas McLemore, and they were the parents of Shelby M. Whitehead (1833), Tillman R. Whitehead (1835-1908), Mary Whitehead (1836-1887), James Whitehead (1838), Catherine Virginia Whitehead (1843-1903), William Henry Whitehead, Sr., (1843-1912), and Margret Whitehead (1845). This family lived in Rankin County, Mississippi, in 1845 according to the Mississippi 1845 State Census Index. Dorcas died in 1870 and John died at an unknown date.

According to "Laurene" [at laurene777@yahoo.com], Betsey's sister was Martha Elizabeth. Further research has found that Martha's middle name was Ann, and she married Arthur Guy (or Gay). They lived in Lauderdale County, Mississippi, and had at least three children: Martha Elizabeth (who married a Mr. Etheridge); William Gay; and Mary A. Gay. Martha died on March 3, 1898, in Tunnel Hill, Mississippi.

On January 24, 1832, **Elizabeth (Betsey) Whitehead** married Jack W. Byrd. Jack had been previously married and was the father of three children, William "Will" N. Byrd, Thomas "Tom" Byrd, and Ann Byrd. Tom died as a young man, but there is no record of the date of his death. In the 1850 US Census William is listed as 21 years of age, but according to family history, he also "died in early manhood." Daughter Ann married Mr. Hinton and moved to Texas before 1850. [Information from Hugh Byrd].

Jack and Betsey had three children. Edward Luton Byrd was born in 1837, blind from birth, but outlived both parents. James Byrd was born in 1835. He valiantly fought as a Confederate soldier and was killed in the fight at Resaca, Georgia. John King Byrd was born on December 24, 1833, a year after his parents married. His story is told in detail in *Traveling Companions*, a book by this author.

Little is known about the life and times of Jack and Betsey Byrd. They lived on a farm in Covington County, Mississippi, and owned about 700 acres of land. They may have lived with their son John King and his wife Malissa for a time, or vice versa. Their home was in the Ocoha community in 1870 but there is no evidence of the homesite today. On the 1860 US Census Adaline Roleigus was a fourteen-year-old who lived with the Byrd family. There is no indication what her role in the family was. She might have been a hired helper.

It is interesting to note that John and Mary Whitehead are also listed on the 1860 Census as neighbors of the Byrd family. John and Mary Whitehead were both born in Georgia, like Betsey, and could have been related to Betsey.

There is no mention of Betsey in the 1880 census and her husband is listed as a widower. What caused her death is unknown, as is her place of burial.

Jack Byrd lived until sometime after 1880. He and his blind son, Edward Byrd, lived as boarders with Frank and Anna Campbell. Jack was 85 years old on the 1880 census and Edward was 40. It is not known why Jack and Edward did not live with J. K. and Malissa Byrd, but perhaps it was because there were five children in the J.K. household by this time, and there might not have been room for an elderly father and blind sibling.

Jack Byrd died after 1880, but cause of death and location of his grave are unknown. There is a U.S. General Land Office Record for December 20, 1890, for Edward L. Byrd. He apparently purchased land in Covington County, but the circumstances surrounding this purchase are unknown.

Since Betsey Whitehead married Jack W. Byrd, she is the link that connects the Whitehead family with the Byrd family.

Sources:

Covington Crossroads by Gwen Keys Hitt (Hattiesburg: University of
   Southern Mississippi Printing Center, 1985)
Mississippi Territorial Census 1805, 1810, 1818
Mississippi State Census 1845
U. S. Census 1820, 1830, 1840, 1850, 1860, 1870, 1880
U. S. General Land Office Records, 1776-2015
Ancestry.com Searches for: James Whitehead, Sr., Charity West and
Wiggins, John Whitehead, Elizabeth "Betsey" Whitehead, James
Whitehead, Jr.
Ancestry.com: U.S. Compiled Service Records, Post-Revolutionary War
Volunteer Soldiers, 1784-1811 and Census of Pensioners, Mississippi –
Southern District
Emails from laurene777@yahoo.com via Nita Byrd Lumpkin and
robert.e.caskey@gte.net via Nita Byrd Lumpkin
Family Papers and Information from Hugh M. Byrd
Personal On-site Visits to Covington County, Mississippi.

www.ingramcontent.com/pod-product-compliance
Lightning Source LLC
LaVergne TN
LVHW051232080426
835513LV00016B/1548